EMOTIONAL INTELLIGENCE

2 books in 1:

How to stop worrying and find unlimited happiness + Emotional Quotient 2.0:

For a better, happier, and healthier life, and success at work.

ALEXANDER W. ALLEN

ISBN: 9798611870679

Under no circumstances will any blame or legal responsibility be held against the publisher, or author, for any damages, reparation, or monetary loss due to the information contained within this book. Either directly or indirectly.

Legal Notice:

This book is copyright protected. This book is only for personal use. You cannot amend, distribute, sell, use, quote or paraphrase any part, or the content within this book, without the consent of the author or publisher.

Disclaimer Notice:

Please note the information contained within this document is for educational and entertainment purposes only. All effort has been executed to present accurate, up to date, and reliable, complete information. No warranties of any kind are declared or implied. Readers acknowledge that the author is not engaging in the rendering of legal, financial, medical or professional advice. The content within this book has been derived from various sources. Please consult a licensed professional before attempting any techniques outlined in this book.

By reading this document, the reader agrees that under no circumstances is the author responsible for any losses, direct or indirect, which are incurred as a result of the use of information contained within this document, including, but not limited to, errors, omissions, or inaccuracies.

TABLE OF CONTENTS

BOOK 1: HOW TO STOP WORRYING AND FIND UNLIMITED HAPPINESS

Overcome Anxiety, Fear, and Stress.

Manage Emotions and Your Social Relationships.

Increase Your Emotional Resilience.

Start Living the Life You Want.

INTRODUCTION

Have you ever been so worried that this emotion alone made you even more worried?

The constant stress, fear, and anxiety you feel can be incredibly draining. In an ideal world, we'd be able to live a peaceful life without having to constantly worry over every little thing. In some instances, you might discover that you are so worried, it feels strange once you don't have anything legitimate to worry over. Some individuals will even go as far as to look for something to worry about because it is such a comfortable state for people to be constantly stressed.

Comfortable doesn't mean happy.

To live a healthy lifestyle where you can actually enjoy this great earth and wonderful life, it's time to understand how we can decrease our worry. It seems if someone were to magically deposit money into your bank account or provide you with a completely new mind or body, all your problems would go away. Unfortunately, good looks and money won't always be the key to happiness.

There is a lot more involved, and it all starts

within your head.

The aim of this discussion will be to help you understand most of the negative emotions that affect your life originate only from a wrong view of yourself and the world around you. The feelings and emotions we have can seem natural, but they don't have to be. This worried life isn't just "The way it is." It is the way that our brain thinks and, luckily, we can start to change that.

From this point of view, it can be understood that overcoming these negative emotions is simply because the change must start from oneself. When you can work on various aspects of your life, it will help to motivate and push you through your biggest mental struggles. There is no quick fix or light switch type trigger that will automatically grant you the life that you want. It takes a bit of time to try to turn your thoughts around, but it can be done. As soon as you take the journey toward reducing your stress, it can be like a weight off your shoulders.

Sometimes we pretend as though nothing is wrong and will instead try to focus on other things. Distracting yourself from the problem is a lot simpler than trying to confront your deepest and darkest feelings. However, if we consistently do this, then it only makes the problem worse. It will start to grow more intense until it's a big heavy pit on our stomachs.

Stress isn't something that just exists within your mind. We can experience stress in every part of our body, depending on how it manifests itself. Throughout this book, we are going to help you to understand worry in every aspect. It will begin by understanding what stress is. We will help you recognize that the mechanisms that cause stress can also be what helps you turn your thoughts around. We'll discuss everything from fear, stress, and anxiety, anger, and low self-esteem.

We can begin to rewire our brains and stop the physical symptoms of stress. You'll be able to distinguish between the real and the imaginary fears that you have. You'll discover passion and motivation within yourself so that you can start to decrease your procrastination and increase the motivation that you feel. You can develop positive thoughts and control your emotions. It will ensure that you improve your relationships.

No longer do you have to live with the fear and stress over what someone else thinks about you. Rather than letting the thoughts of many roll through your mind, you can focus only on growing the incredible thoughts that you have as an individual. Stress isn't something that we have to be afraid of. We can figure out how to use it for good!

We are not only able to provide you with motivation, but we also want to help you understand the mechanisms that generate negative emotions, as well as the tools needed to overcome them. There are many mental and practical things that you can start to do so that you can get the right mindset.

Before getting started, there are a few things that you have to understand to be ready for this journey. Be open-minded and willing to admit that some of your thoughts aren't healthy. Accept that you might have handled emotions in an unhealthy way in the past. Recognize how your thoughts and feelings played a role in creating the person that you have become. Be willing to come face to face with yourself and work through the most difficult things that are felt.

We might touch on some more difficult subjects within these texts such as trauma or emotional challenges. Ensure that you give yourself a break if needed because it is not always a piece of cake to have to work through your emotions. You are a powerful individual with a great mind that is capable of anything you put your focus on.

Worry seems so normal, so why do you have to stop worrying about improving your life?

You deserve to have a worry-free mind. You should be able to go to the store without getting stressed. You deserve to enjoy work even on the worst days. Fixing problems should be like a puzzle that brings you joy—not something that makes you sick to your stomach. We deserve to go to parties and have fun with friends. It is okay to spend a little extra money sometimes or act on impulse. You don't have to stress over things that are out of your control.

Free yourself from this restraining emotion. Recognize the way that it has taken a grip on your life. It might seem uncomfortable to let go of the stress since it can be a constant in your life you can depend on. Recognize your individuality and worth and accept that you don't have to live like this. We will help you along the way to ensure that you always have the mental tools you need.

What is important in recognizing first is that you are in charge of what happens next. The power to change your brain already exists within your own mind.

UNDERSTANDING WORRY

The mechanisms that regulate our emotions are similar to the mechanisms that are needed to overcome them. When you have a worried thought, it is something that exists within your brain. You are experiencing a cognitive distortion, a mental block, or an unhealthy thinking pattern. It is one connection in your brain that occurs that makes it hard to see things clearly.

When you are thinking healthy, the same thing happens. Our brains are filled with neurons that create connections called synapses. These connections are things that are created each time that we learn something new. When you are learning information that is new to you, it is likely based on things that you understand already.

Your brain builds on itself and becomes stronger and stronger. Unfortunately, some of our brains experience things that make those connections result in more negative thoughts. It is not as if these thoughts are bad; they simply make going through our day-to-day activities much more difficult.

While it might not necessarily be wrong to think about how you don't like spending time around people, that doesn't make your customer service job any easier.

When we don't manage worry, it can cause thought patterns that are difficult. However, we can actually turn those exact thoughts and make them positive. With practice and the right mental conditioning, we can enable our brains to continue to create those healthy connections, but rather than allowing them to continually produce negative thoughts, we can create productive ones.

It's not a matter of shutting the bad out. We will simply use those worried thoughts and find the good from them. We can use our emotions and feelings to better get a sense of our world and what's around us. The better you have emotional management over yourself, the easier it is to navigate through this world (Cherry, 2019).

How the Brain Mechanisms Work

By far, your brain is the most incredible organ within your body. Of course, it's pretty crazy to think about your heart that pumps blood throughout your systems, or a stomach that processes tasty food. Out of everything that exists within us, however, our brain is the most complex. With this brain, we have the ability to think of new ideas. We can solve problems and we can have fun conversations with people that we love. At the same time, we can use these brains to feel pretty awful.

We might become really sad for no reason and have burst of crying fits. We might fight with people only to realize afterward that we were completely in the wrong for even being an angry and first place. We can build so much intense rage within our brains that it can cause us to do things that we regret immensely. There is no doubt that this mushy pink organ is filled with wonder. The biggest struggle that many of us have is because our brain is worried.

What is worry? The things that scare some people are just so meaningless to others. The thing about understanding worry is that we don't fully know how to define it. When we can't figure things out in our brain, then it can cause us to feel really lost. When we don't fully grasp how something works, or the inner mechanisms, then it can make us really frustrated.

How many times were you simply in a bad mood without understanding? Why did you find yourself frequently feeling exhausted, but there is nothing that you could pinpoint as being a cause for this feeling? When it comes to some emotions, they can be pretty easy to figure out. If you are broken up with your significant other, then you are probably going to cry and be really sad. If you lose a loved one and they end up passing away, that's another obvious reason why you might be upset. When you struggle at work and feel overwhelmed by school, then you are certainly going to be dealing with some hard emotions.

At the same time, we have to recognize that just because we don't understand how we feel doesn't mean that it's just some sort of mystical element within your brain. There is going to be an underlying thing that helps you recognize what a greater issue might be that you are struggling with.

To understand your worry, let's first try to recognize what your brain is. Everything that we have ever learned about the human brain has been done so through the use of a human brain. Even if we might use computer technology to help us determine statistical information, it is still the human brain that created the program. It is still the human brain that decides which analytics will be recorded, and what data might matter or not.

The human brain is the control center of your body. It is like what exists under a car's hood. It is the computer and not the monitor on the desktop that you use to study or read. Your brain is everything. Without your brain, you would be nothing. Of course, other organs play just as an important role in our bodies. If you lost your stomach or your heart, this is going to be a lot harder for you to survive. However, you can still survive without your own version of a heart.

For example, you could get a heart transplant. The brain is different. The brain isn't just a machine that helps our body function. It is what makes us who we are. If you were to have a brain transplant, you would be a different person. Of course, that's not possible, but perhaps one day it could be. What would that look like?

Think back to the 60s and a time where people were given lobotomies as a medical procedure. The idea behind a lobotomy is that it might fix certain things wrong with a person's personality. Now, when we talk about 'wrong,' that's a completely subjective term.

Of course, in the 60s, it was definitely something stricter. It used to be wrong for women to be a little bit more outgoing or have a strong opinionated voice. It used to be wrong to be homosexual. In history, we used lobotomies to try to fix these 'problems.' What ended up happening is that we took the personality of the person away. They would use a needle to scramble a certain part of the patient's brain, and in turn, that would leave a drooling, blubbering zombie. Some people were able to fully function afterward, but they were not the same person that they were before going into the procedure. We understand now that there isn't one specific part of your brain that is responsible for creating who you are. It is a complex network of systems.

To break it down, simply recognize first how you have a left side and the right side of your brain; the left side is a little bit more logical. This is where the reasoning happens within your brain. The right side is more creative. This is where you will think of new ideas and make connections. These two parts alone create a harmonious blend that encapsulates the person that you are. Now you don't have to fully understand neuroscience to recognize what might cause you worry. This is just an example of how different parts of your brain are variant, but still work together for an overall poetic function.

To break it down simply, we have to understand that stress is a reaction within all animals, and many living things too. There is a fight or flight response. What this refers to is how when we are presented with something that causes us stress, we will react to it either by fighting it off or running away from it. Imagine that you came in contact with a very angry dog.

If you went up to this dog and you started trying to fight it, the dog is going to fight back. At the same time, this dog might also recognize that you are in control, and rather than fighting back, they might simply run from you. This is the case for many animals. Most aggressive animals will try to fight. Think of things like lions, or spiders or snakes, they would try to bite you. Then there are other animals, like birds or bunnies, or deer that are a little bit gentler. When they're approached with the stress, they're more likely to run away.

Human beings have this response in a similar way. When they're scared, they will either try to fight or they will run away. Just because you are presented with something that is not a physical stressor does not mean that you won't still have this reaction. When something presents itself to you as stressful, such as a problem at work, then you are going to react in the same way. You will either react by fighting it off, which could be a confrontation with somebody, or you will run away from it. This could be seen in the way that you might go to the bar after work and have a few drinks to try to forget your problems.

Now, that doesn't mean that every single issue we have we always react that way. That is just usually the first response. What we are going to do in this book is to help guide you away from that animalistic reaction. Before getting into that, we have to understand that stress is perfectly normal and it's completely healthy. When you do have a stress, you can choose to fight it in a healthy way. You can choose to run from it in a healthy way too.

For example, let's say that you get an eviction notice. Maybe you fell behind on rent because of some other issues in your life, and now you are going to be losing your apartment. You could fight this in a few ways. You could fight it by being angry, belligerent, and causing more issues. You could also fight it by sending a letter to your landlord and telling them of your issues. You can be honest with them and very apologetic. You can use a forgiving tone and work out a deal to pay back the rent over the next few months, in addition to the rent that you would already be paying. That would be a healthy way that you could fight it.

You could also run from it. You could run from it by abandoning your apartment and living on the streets, only falling into even more toxic patterns. You could flip it in a healthy way by making sure that you get a new, cheaper apartment that you can afford, and deal with the situation of eviction that was presented to you. We all have choices, and we have to recognize that there are certain things out of our control. Our emotions are always going to be within our power. Your reaction is the way that you will choose to respond to a situation action. For example, if somebody punches you in the face, then it is perfectly normal for you to be upset over this. It is not okay to just physically hit other people. At the same time, we have to recognize that there are multiple responses that you can have. You could simply respond by walking away. You can respond by punching them back.

The reaction you have is different from the emotion that you feel from that. These are the basic steps of psychology that you should understand as we get into some deeper things, which will help you recognize your worry and how you can overcome it. Remember that this is not something easy. You've built a life around fear, stress, anxiety, anger, depression, and low self-esteem. Your intensity of that emotion is subjective, but by seeking out a book to help you alleviate these feelings, it's clear worry plays an enormous role in your life.

It took a while to build that, so it's going to take a bit to break down. It certainly won't take as long because acknowledging it is the first part and that can be a huge relief.

Imagine that you bought a new home and there was a big ugly statue in the backyard garden. Everything about this yard was beautiful, but you had to walk past the disgusting gargoyle statue in the middle of it. Every time you try to enjoy the scenery of the garden, you are reminded of this big ugly gargoyle. The first step in relief from this is buying the sledgehammer to destroy it. You thought about listing it for sale or even giving it away for free, but you decided that it's so ugly that no one should have to deal with it at all.

You buy the sledgehammer–the first acknowledgement that it's time to do something about this eyesore. Then you destroy it. You come face to face with this challenge and you don't have to worry about looking at this ever again. The first hit feels great, but it's harder than you thought. The force of the statue against your grip around the sledgehammer makes your knuckles sore. It is a lot more work than you thought it'd be, but each hit gets easier and easier. Every time you manage to take the sledgehammer and destroy a part of the statue, a sense of relief washes over you.

Eventually the statue is destroyed, and the wrecked pieces lay beneath you. That's enough for the day, so you leave, happy that the statue is destroyed. There are still pieces you have to pick up, and some of the stone bits will never fully be picked up from the ground and the grass of your garden. No matter how long the clean-up takes, you'll just be relieved you never have to look at this gargoyle again.

Your worry is the gargoyle, and your garden is your brain. There will always be remnants of this struggle you've been dealing with, but no longer do you have to worry about staring it in the face every day.

It will still take some time, and you will have moments when you go back to old patterns of thinking. At the end of the day, what's more important than anything else is that you are doing your best to pay special attention to your thoughts and feelings. Let's now take a deeper look at the most challenging emotions that you feel (Cherry,

2019).

Fear, Stress, and Anxiety

It seems like in our society, everybody is always stressed out. You see stress balls in many stores, stress-relieving tea, and plenty of soothing products like massagers or meditation tapes.

Stress is completely normal. Is it the thing that causes you to panic all the time, but it's not something that has to necessarily be bad. It is usually our thoughts that will lead you into that afterward. There are three stages to the worry that we have. There's fear, stress, and anxiety. Let's discuss first what fear is.

Fear is what you are afraid of. This could be anything from lions, tigers and bears, to simply being afraid to call a restaurant to order a pizza. Fear is something that is 100% subjective. There are common fears that we share among each other, but at the same time, we have to recognize that the individual will have their own things that make them fearful. When recognizing fear, we have to understand the basic human instincts that we have and the things that we might have experienced through our life which created that initial worry.

The symptoms of fear include:

- fear of something specific—losing

control, dying, fainting, etc.

- nausea
- sweating
- increased heart beat
- shortness of breath
- dizziness
- the feeling like you might be choking

Fear over spiders, creepy crawly animals, and other threatening creatures is completely normal. A lot of these things, like snakes or spiders, could be venomous and could kill us. It is a natural instinct to not want to cuddle up in bed next to a big hairy tarantula. When it comes to other fears, like heights or the darkness, these also are natural because as humans we self-preserve. At the end of the day, our instinct is to simply survive.

Of course, eating, making money, making friends and having a fun life seem instinctual things to us, in a sense, but at the end of the day, the number one priority that we have, biologically, is to protect ourselves. When you go walking on the edge of a cliff, that natural instinct kicks in and tells you, "Hey, stop doing this because you might die." It's as simple as that. When we're in the dark, that kind of limits your senses, so it's harder to prepare yourself if there was an attack. If you get trapped in a room with a bear, obviously, having the light on would make that a lot less scary than being in the dark.

These are natural things that not just humans fear, but other animals can be known to have stress over too. Then there are fears that are created within us. These are fears like being alone, losing your job, never succeeding in life, always being poor, and so on. All of these fears can attach themselves back to one of those basic instincts, but we also have to recognize that in our society, we definitely create a lot of fear. For example, the beauty standards that we put on people can cause worry. You are expected to be perfectly thin, with flawless skin, gorgeous flowing hair, and the best style. When we lack one of these things, it can cause fear.

Now, fear is normal, and is actually healthy. Though it might be something that you struggle to have that exists inside of you, that can be good for you because it motivates you. Fear reminds you of what is important. It helps you pinpoint the struggles that you have in your life so that you can work on those weaknesses and turn them into your strengths.

Moving on to the next tier comes stress. Stress is also something that's healthy. Stress is when we have that kind of fear but prolonged. Stress is normal because, again, it is a motivator. When you are stressed about paying your bills, then you have to work. When you are stressed about finding somebody that you love, then you improve on your physical appearance and your personality so that you can attract other people These kinds of stresses are normal, and we have to accept them as an everyday part of life.

The symptoms of stress include:

- disconnect from reality
- indigestion and gastrointestinal issues
- fast beating heart
- sweat, especially in the palms
- shaking
- dizziness
- muscle soreness
- teeth grinding
- restlessness

To think about being a happy person who is never going to experience stress again– that's just simply never going to happen. Even the richest, most attractive people who seemingly have it all will still have stress; it is wired into our body.

Anxiety is the third level. Anxiety is when stress goes unmanaged for so long that it turns into something chronic. There are different kinds of anxieties that people can have. You might have generalized anxiety. This would be something that just causes you to always react in an anxious way rather than processing new stressors. Then you might react based on emotion, immediately. Perhaps you are going on a trip with someone and then the plans change last minute. Though the plans aren't necessarily changing into something negative, that kind of unexpected alteration of what you were expecting can cause you to react in a stressful way. Some individuals will also experience social anxiety. This is when they have a fear of the public or other people and are not able to interact and socialize in a normal, healthy way. Your anxiety can be specified based on your personality, but it can also just be basically who you are. Every little thing might make you anxious and every little thing might bother you doesn't always make sense. It is still something that you know is true and that you know is there. Generalized anxiety is very real, and that's something that we have to start to recognize. It can show it soft and crazy ways in our body.

The symptoms of anxiety include:

- constant worrying
- agitation/annoyance
- rapid heartbeat
- shakiness/dizziness
- nausea/vomiting
- fatigue/lethargy
- memory and concentration issues

- sore and tense muscles
- clenched and aching jaw

As you can see between the three types of worrying, they have some similarities. The differentiation between these is the intensity in which these symptoms are felt. The more that these symptoms affect your life, the easier it is to tell with which you struggle. For example, if you can't handle leaving your home without shaking, that's a sign you probably have anxiety. If you only shake when giving big presentations, that's just normal fear or stress.

We don't want to completely eliminate this from our life because it is a normal part of who we are. What we do want to do is make sure that we start to regulate it. Fear, stress, and anxiety are the basic things that you will experience. After you have these chronic feelings, it can result in that anger issues, depression, and having low self-esteem. Let's take a look now at some of those more challenging emotions so that you can get a good sense of the things that you are actually feeling.

Anger and Depression

Anger is something so easily felt. You stub your toe on the corner of the table. The line at the coffee shop you normally go to is taking 10 minutes extra. Somebody cut you off in traffic. They don't have your size shirt at the store. Your favorite TV show just got canceled. The internet isn't working. Your phone is going too slow. They gave you the wrong food when you ordered delivery.

These simple things can cause so much anger. Then there's the really big stuff. You found out that your partner has been cheating on you. The person you hate at work got the job that you wanted. Everybody who you graduated high school with is already married with kids, and you still can't remember to have clean underwear in your dresser.

Anger is common, it's real, and it's normal to have. Anybody in the world can have anger.

Anger is something that feels awful, and we don't always know *why* we have it. It seriously can feel as if your blood is boiling. Anger can blind you. You might find that you were in a fit of rage when you are so angry because you simply don't understand what's going on around you. The first thing to understand about anger is that it is a secondary emotion. This means that there is a feeling that you have before even dealing with anger.

This anger is usually a sign that there's something hidden from deeper within. For example, you might feel guilt, annoyance, grumpiness, overwhelmed, grief, fear, and so on. All of these emotions could potentially lead to anger when you are not properly managing them.

Anger can cause us to feel intense emotions, even greater than what we are already experienced when we are so mad. Think of your emotional state like a soda bottle. The more you shake the bottle, the bigger is going to explode as soon as you open the cap. Of course, if you let the anger cool down for a minute, then the cap won't explode upon opening. At the same time, we have to consider that anger is also something that will simply blow the lid right off. Even when you do open that soda finally, it's going to be a lot different than when you bought it before it was shaken. It'll be flat and a different consistency because you altered it so much through the experiences that you have.

What we have to recognize about anger is that it's not going to go away if we ignore it. Instead, it's going to build. It is like an infected wound. You can put a Band-Aid on it, but if the infection exists, it will still be there underneath the Band-Aid. You might not see the infection, but that's because it's spreading through your bloodstream. Anger does the same thing. It will seep into every aspect of your life. If you have constant anger at work, then you are going to bring that home with you. It will turn into anger toward your family. So frequently we don't recognize the underlying emotion or thought that drives the anger, which is why it keeps coming back. If you pull the weed from the top, then you are ignoring the root and it will continue to grow. To really get that weed out of your garden you have to dig it out from the root and destroy it. That's what we have to do with our anger. Since it is a secondary emotion, that means it is a reaction to stress.

When you feel angry, you have to figure out what you are stressed about. You have to look at the things that are causing you so much anxiety and decide how you are going to resolve it to not have to feel that consistent anger.

Moving on, depression can be a result of long-term unmanaged anger. Sigmund Freud believed that depression was anger turned inward.

After experiencing such frequent anger all the time, it can be easy for many individuals to undergo constant depressive states because of the thoughts that they have. When you are more of a passive person that doesn't mean that you are not angry.

When it comes to anger, we often have a stereotype around what that looks like. We envision some big guy with muscles, a bulging red face, and fists swinging. That is not true at all. Anger exists even within the most innocent and purest people. Think of children, they get angry all the time! You might see a little girl skipping down the street with pigtails and a dress. She might smile at you and look so cute, but what you don't realize is that 10 minutes earlier, she had a tantrum so bad, she punched her mom in the face and ripped out a lock of hair. These tiny humans still have anger just as intense as that big, raging man could. Everybody has anger, and it just presents itself in different ways.

When people are a little bit more passive or gentle in their nature, then they might discover that this turns into depression. When we can't take our anger out on other people, then we direct that in ourselves. This can destroy our self-esteem and cause us to experience chronic depression. Depression leaves you feeling hopeless, and as if there's nothing you can do.

Depression is another mental struggle that you might discover you have. It can all start with a simple worry and build on top of itself until it becomes a festering wound within your heart and your mind. Of course, it's not physically in your heart, but being depressed is definitely a compassion killer. It can be hard to find any sort of motivation or joy when you constantly experienced depression. It can have similar symptoms to anxiety in the fact that you might discover you have irregular heartbeats higher blood pressure and more anxious behavior. The thing about depression is that sometimes it can be like anxiety but seemingly more relaxed. This is only on the outside, however, because inside your mind being depressed doesn't always mean having lethargic thoughts. We often think of a depressed individual as somebody who just lays around all day and seems mopey or sad.

It's so much more complex than this. There are definitely cases of people who suffer from depression who might be stuck in bed and struggle to do things physically, but you can also have high functioning depressed individuals who do manage to get up and go to work every day and continue to live a seemingly normal life while still being hopelessly depressed on the inside.

Depression can show itself through feelings and thoughts of confusion. When you are depressed, it's really hard to understand what your emotions are. In one instance, you can go from being extremely anxious and fearful of death, and then 30 seconds later, you can want to die and have suicidal thoughts.

There's no one way to be depressed, but it is something that we don't always fully recognize. Part of this is because of the stigma, and then the other part is because many people simply don't think that they're depressed because they might be more hyperactive.

Depression will be a loss of interest. You'll lack the desires that you used to. If you are somebody who used to love playing guitar, painting, exercising and doing other fun social activities, you might discover that not only have you stopped doing these, but you simply have no desire to do them all.

Anger will play into depression because it can cause rage. You might discover that you start to feel extra anxious and frustrated with the world. That's completely normal because your emotions are so high and erratic that you won't have clarity. It will inhibit your ability to fully understand situations and have a healthy outlook on life.

Those who constantly struggle with depression or anxiety will likely have low self-esteem. Let's take a look at what that means and how it presents itself within different individuals (Pratt, 2014).

Low Self-Esteem

Having low self-esteem is a constant struggle.

You are with yourself all day long, so being in a place where you can't stand yourself is incredibly challenging. It is exhausting to have low self-esteem because it's like you are your own bully in some instances. If you have low self-esteem, then your struggle to feel good about yourself most of the time. Low self-esteem can happen to anybody, whether they're the picture-perfect example of what attractive is, or if they are like a hideous monster. Self-esteem doesn't matter who it takes over, but when it does, it is a constant toxic struggle.

Having low self-esteem is usually pretty easy to identify in some individuals. You might struggle because you don't like the way that you look, you might have insecurities about your body, your hair, your clothes, your face, your skin, your teeth, and other common things like that.

It's very normal to dislike the body that we're in. There are some other effects of having a very low self-esteem that we don't always really understand. We often overlook the symptoms and won't frequently even think of them as being a symptom of low self-esteem.

The one thing that people with low self-esteem will struggle with is their ability to trust themselves. Have you ever found yourself in the middle of a grocery store, completely lost because you can't decide whether you should buy red or green apples? Maybe you can't figure out if you should have angel hair or regular spaghetti for dinner. Perhaps it's choosing between 1% and 2% milk that leaves you completely paralyzed. Simple decisions like this we should be able to make without second guessing ourselves, but those who have low self-esteem won't be able to trust their gut. They'll constantly be looking at the decisions they made, and they'll be really hard on themselves for choosing potentially the wrong thing. Those with low self-esteem will also always overthink everything, whether it's a quick comment that somebody made to you or, again, a decision you made.

You will probably overthink it until is transformed into a completely new thought. For example, if somebody comments on your hair one day, you might be so insecure about this that you believe they are actually attacking you, when really they simply just told you that they liked your hair. People with low self-esteem will not be able to take compliments because they will overthink it to a point that it becomes an insult. If somebody told you that you were looking good one day, then you would take that as a hint that you didn't look good the rest of the days. It is not necessarily that one compliment means other negatives are true.

You will also overthink the choices that you have to make to the point that you might not even make that decision at all. Perhaps you get invited to a party one night and you can't decide if you want to go. You keep thinking about how you want it to just stay home and watch a movie, but you're feeling guilty about skipping out on the party. You're afraid of what you might miss. You might sit there all night, trying to consider whether you should go, only to find that the party started two hours ago. At that point, you decide there's no point in going. If you were able to have a high self-esteem and actually trust your gut, you wouldn't have to worry so much about whether you made the right decision.

Simply choosing what to watch at night can be really hard for people with low self-esteem. You might have to sit there and look for a movie to pick out for three hours, when in reality you could have watched two different movies already. Choosing an outfit for the day is probably incredibly difficult for you because your mind is really good at always looking for something that is wrong.

Those who have a low self-esteem will be incredibly hard on themselves. They will always look for a way to make a mean comment about the things that they did. You might think that it's bad to get a B on a test, but if your friend does, you congratulate them and tell them it was a good job. At the same time, those with low self-esteem don't hold themselves to the same standards as others. This means that your standards are going to be a lot higher for yourself. Perhaps you constantly think that you are overweight or you just simply hate the shape of your body, but at the same time, you might not ever judge anybody else's body and you don't really think it's that big of a deal to be overweight.

Sometimes the lower the self-esteem, the

harder you are on yourself, and the less challenging that you are on other people. This isn't always the case. Of course, sometimes we do have such a low self-esteem because we are so judgmental of other people; therefore, the judgment on yourself is tripled or more.

If you were taught to be a judgmental person, maybe by your parents, older siblings or just society in general, then maybe you are frequently holding others to a high standard. Usually what ends up happening is that you will be extra hard on yourself because not only do you have to live up to your expectations that you have for other people, but you actually have to exceed it in the end.

You will probably have a lot of emotional turmoil. This means that whenever you feel something, you'll feel it deeply. If somebody makes a comment about the way you look, and you take it negatively. It could be something that ruins not only that moment, but the next week, because you can't stop thinking about it.

Sometimes those with low self-esteem will be too attached to their work. It can almost be at an unhealthy level. Most animals have a certain esteem that they need to fill. This esteem just simply means having a purpose. Esteem is respect and admiration, acknowledgement of your worth. And it's a validation that you are a good person. We can sometimes even see esteem in animals. For example, if you were in a room of people and there was one dog, and the dog did something funny and everybody laughed at the dog, then it almost seems as though it's embarrassed. Of course, this dog doesn't experience embarrassment the same way that humans do, but some experts believe they can experience shame (Ward, n.d.).

Of course, we really can't understand how animals feel, but we do know that pack and group type animals, like dogs and humans, need to feel accepted by others. This isn't just a social thing, but it is actually a survival skill. We are a tribe kind of species in that we need other people to survive. Back before we could just go to the grocery store and get different food, we were a hunter and gatherer society. Some people were better at certain things, and others excelled in the opposite area. You work together harmoniously within a group to live a fulfilled life. Of course, we can be independent people and you don't need others to have a happy life. At the same time, we can't overlook the way that our instincts tell us that we have a certain esteem that needs to be filled. This is why having a job can really boost your self-esteem. It is not necessarily that you're passionate about the work that you're doing, but to have a task and complete it successfully is a boost in your ego. It reminds you that you do have worth and it validates the person that you are in this world.

This is why if you hate yourself, you're continually challenging yourself, and you never really appreciate your worth, you might pour yourself into the work or the school work that you have because that is where you find your purpose. When we break ourselves down all the time, we're just draining our own identity. By doing this, we lack the ability to find validation from ourselves, so we will constantly look for it and other places. This is why you might realize that many people who are obsessed with social media and are constantly posting pictures of themselves, might actually be more insecure than somebody who never posts at all. It might seem like somebody who is constantly taking pictures of themselves has an extremely high level of confidence, but there are certain individuals who do have low self-esteem and are seeking that external validation because they can't find it within themselves.

There are a few reasons why you might have such a low self-esteem. The first one is your childhood. Look back to the way that you were raised. Did you have extremely strict parents who were always really hard on you? Were you somebody who frequently experienced emotional abuse, or even neglect? When you weren't given the chance to fulfill that esteem as a child, then as an adult, you're going to seek it more so than others.

Constantly being berated, made fun of, or made to feel like you were stupid as a child is a huge way to kill your self-esteem. If you were somebody who was frequently punished for the things that you did, and even the thoughts that you had, of course, you're going to be lacking confidence now. It is not just a matter of punishing you for doing something wrong, but many parents shame their children for being less intelligent. For example, you might have had somebody yell at you when you got the homework question wrong as you were doing homework together. It is okay to get questions wrong, and it's okay to say silly or dumb things, but we can't make people feel bad because of this. It simply destroys their self-esteem. Neglect is also something that could cause you to have a low self-esteem. As children, we still have that certain level of validation that we need from other people, and it's something our parents should provide us with. It is as simple as telling your children that you love them, and showing them compassion through hugs, kisses, rewards, and other validating small acts of kindness. When we didn't receive any of that whatsoever, then that means that we had to find net worth on our own, and not everybody is struggling enough to do this.

It's incredibly challenging to build your own motivation from the ground up, so it's perfectly normal for many individuals who experienced neglect in their childhood to have a low self-esteem. Now, if you experienced bullying in school, then this is another way that your esteem is probably incredibly low. Bullying is one of the hardest things to deal with, aside from parental abuse, because those are our peers who are supposed to be validating us. When you go to a new space, like a school, then it's a completely different social environment that should be accepting and open. When instead, we get punished for being ourselves, it will completely destroy our ability to have a positive character.

Childhood sets the standard for how you act as an adult so if your self-esteem was destroyed then, it's going to be destroyed now. In the next few chapters, we're going to provide you with coping mechanisms, but it's important that you recognize where your low self-esteem might have come from. Was it a mother or a father who was an extremely hard on you? Did you have other parental figures such as grandparents or aunts and uncles who are constantly berating you? Even older siblings and friends could have been the reason that you hate yourself so much now. Often, that just comes from ourselves. Society can create extremely high standards, and when we don't live up to them, then it can be damaging to our ego. Consider all these factors when you're trying to determine what the root of your low self-esteem issues might be

(Kominos, A).

How We Can Rewire Our Brains

What we have to recognize is that even though you might experience some of these emotions and they seem so obvious to you, it can be difficult to put our feelings and our emotions into words. Going over these symptoms you might have discovered that you had things you didn't even associate with anxiety. In the next chapter, we're going to start to provide you with more specific things that you're experiencing so that you can better recognize how to pinpoint your anxiety and target it specifically. If we just treat worry, anxiety, fear, anger, depression, and so on, all like it's the same thing, then we will not always heal properly. Sometimes you have to break your issues down and really look at the root so that you can discover how the best way to kill off that root.

Now that you're aware of all these different types of issues that can stem from worry, you might be wondering if this is something that you're stuck with forever. We've already touched on the fact that worry doesn't just simply go away. You're always going to experience stress. In the same instance, you have to recognize that this does not mean that you have to live in misery. Stress, does not equate to a bad life. Stress is simply a motivator that we can help drive our passion.

This is where neuroplasticity comes in. Neuroplasticity is the way that your brain can change its shape. This doesn't mean that it's going to flip upside-down or turn into a square. We're talking about the way that your brain is organized. Some parts right now are stronger than others, and what we're going to help you do in this book is recognize those strengths and turn them around so that they level themselves out in a healthy and normal way.

When you learn new things, a new neuron is created. The way that you reshape your brain is by consistently bringing in new neurons. You're already aware of what it feels like to be depressed, but you might not fully understand what it is and how it presents itself with in your brain. As you start to learn about those symptoms and causes, then it kind of creates a new neuron that helps you better build the foundation for the tools that you will use to destroy that constant pattern of thinking.

Each time you learn something new, as we already discussed earlier, those neurons connect to something that we already know. You already know what it feels like to be depressed and anxious.

These feelings have formed memories in your brain that you will always respond to. Just as when you learn new information a connection in your brain is formed, having various worried thoughts and emotions can create that connection as well. Rather than forming knowledge around a certain topic, your brain associates a feeling with a situation. This is why those with trauma will experience the same feelings they had in a pressing situation as they experienced at the time of a trauma. Someone who has been injured in a car accident might be triggered by cars, therefore experiencing the same panicked feelings when riding in a moving vehicle that they felt at the time of the initial accident.

You can use these connections that already exist to form stronger emotions around positive thinking. As you learn about mental health, you'll be able to work through some of the negative associations and connections that exist in your mind. It is this way that you will be able to use your mental health to start the healing process.

It forms a stronger knowledge of the subject so that you can better recognize the tools you'll be able to use to strengthen your brain power. This is how we can take lemons and make lemonade—you are using the things that already exist within your brain to heal the pain that is there.

Growth and learning is going to be the most important part of this process.

Take the opportunities that comes to you to

learn more and explore your curiosity. This is a way that your brain is going to put its energy into something new and productive, rather than the constant rumination or worry that you already have.

Let's take a further look at what this anxiety and worry is doing to you now so that you can understand what the root of your problem is. You can't fix the issue if you don't understand what the problem is. It is like trying to take Tylenol to cure cancer. You have to recognize the realistic problem that they're fully understanding so that you can beat it. Of course, when we're talking about something like cancer, there isn't a cure for that yet, but we do know as much as we can in this moment, and we do our best to try and resolve those issues with things like radiation or chemotherapy.

While we might not have the one exact specific tool for your individual worry, we do have the information you need to understand about the root of your problems, along with coping mechanisms in later chapters to help fulfill some of the need to resolve those issues.

WHAT STRESS AND WORRY DOES TO YOUR LIFE

You already know that worry can keep you up at night. It can make you afraid to do the things you used to do and it can keep you from living a normal, happy life. Do you know how it could destroy your stomach or cause back pain? Did you know it can be the reason why you have headaches or issues with grinding your teeth?

There are many other symptoms of stress we might not recognize that we need to make ourselves aware of so we can understand the severity of this problem. For whatever reason in our society, it seems like there is it the ignoring of mental health, whether we overlook childhood trauma or dismiss anxiety as just needing to "chill out."

We don't play as much of a role and mental health as we do the rest of our bodies. What we need to recognize is that going to a psychiatrist or a therapist should be as normal as going to the dentist or a chiropractor. It is completely healthy to seek out a therapist. Even healthy people should be going to a therapist. You still go to the dentist even when you don't have cavities. In this chapter, we're going to remind you that your worry isn't just something that you have to "get over." It's something that can seep into every part of your life. Not everybody is ready to go to a therapist and not everybody even has the health insurance or financial means. We're not going to try to convince you to go see a doctor right now. That's something that you should be deciding on your own, but it's certainly encouraged. In this chapter, instead, we are going to help you see every way that worry can destroy your life.

It is only once you recognize just how intrinsic and toxic this kind of thinking can be that you will fully be ready to move on and never deal with this again.

Physical Symptoms

Stress seems like something that only exists within our mind, but we don't recognize is that it can actually pass through every part of our body. When you are stressed, as we already discussed, it's a flight or fight response that you have. What this means is that your body prepares for anything that could come its way. When the stress levels in your body increase, you actually affect the hormonal balance within your body. Cortisol is a hormone that is specifically found in your body when you are stressed. It is not necessarily a bad thing. It helps increase your heart rate, and it alerts your focus and attention so that you are prepared for anything. Unfortunately, when we experience chronic stress, that means that we overload our body with cortisol. It can have negative effects on every aspect of your body. Not only is that going to alter your chemistry, but we also often keep tense muscles clenched when we are feeling stress or anxiety. That will have negative effects on our health, too.

When you have prolonged chronic stress that you're not taking care of, it could even lead to cardiovascular disease. You might experience high blood pressure, crazy heart rhythms, and you could even have a heart disease. Heart attacks and strokes can also occur within people who don't properly manage their stress.

The hormones in your body can directly affect the hormones regulated in other parts, such as your reproductive health. Biological females who consistently feel stressed out might notice that their menstrual cycles are actually altered. You could end up having a period for months at a time or you could go weeks and weeks without even bleeding at all. It can be a very scary time for women because once your period is irregular, that will make you even more stressed. For example, if you miss your period because of stress, then you might be even more stressed wondering if there is a chance that you could be pregnant. At the same time, when we have a constant menstruation, it makes us feel as though something more serious could be wrong. These hormones could also affect your sexual desires. For men, you might discover that even though you do have sexual urges, you experience erectile dysfunction simply because your hormonal balance is all off. You could also find that you premature ejaculate consistently, simply because of overactive hormones. It really goes either way, depending on what your stress levels are and the other symptoms that you're experiencing.

We can also see stress in our hair and our skin. Some people will even break out in a rash because of stress. You might experience frequent hair loss. If you're noticing when you take a shower or brush your hair that a lot is coming out, then it could be a sign that stress has carried to other parts of your body. You might notice that you have brittle nails that chip easily. This is partially because of irregular hormones. You might also discover that being stressed causes you to pick more. When we are always picking at scabs or popping pimples, it makes the breakout even worse. This can end up causing us more stress and create a vicious cycle of bad skin habits. Constant stress can also lead to gastrointestinal issues. This is anything that might deal with your stomach, your esophagus, and your intestines. Because of cortisol in your stomach, you are also going to affect the hormonal balance within your digestive system. Your digestive system has a lot of bacteria and important flora that regulate hormones within your body. Your stomach is actually a microbiome, in that there are other living organisms within your digestive tract that will make sure to break down food and send minerals and nutrients to the right places.

Your stomach can seem like such a simple organ. You feed it, it processes food and then you get rid of the waste. It is the second stage that is the most complex. You have trillions of bacteria in your stomach that helps to ensure your food is properly being processed. This microbiome is almost as complex as our brain.

Along the way, your stomach goes through a lot to help regulate your hormonal balance. When you're adding extra cortisol on top of everything that can wear and tear away at your belly, you might discover that you have GERD, acid reflux, or ulcerative colitis.

You might struggle with constipation or diarrhea frequently because of your stress. If you notice that you get nervous and feel that in your stomach, then there's a good chance that your stress will be the cause of your digestive issues. Of course, some of us just simply have issues with our digestive system such as irritable bowel syndrome or lactose intolerance. At the same time, we have to remember that stress could be one of the causes for the pain in our gut that we feel.

Anxiety is a little more extreme than stress, and this can make your body feel even worse. You might experience a panic attack from time to time. What this is, is a sudden burst of anxiety that almost paralyzes you. Panic attacks can be really terrifying because it feels almost as if somebody else is in control of your body. Sometimes these attacks are specified to an incident. This would be something that's considered an anxiety attack. An anxiety attack might be if you're confronted with something that you know makes you anxious. It is when you have to come face to face with a phobia. For example, if you have a fear of dogs, and you go for a walk and run into a dog, then you might have an anxiety attack because it's triggered by a specific instance. A panic attack is something that is a little bit more random. You might be sitting in class one day and suddenly begin to cry. Many people think of a panic attack as something where you're screaming and flailing your arms, breathing heavy and vomiting. We often have an image of people having a panic attack as either passing out or huffing and puffing into a brown paper bag. Sometimes you could be sitting completely motionless and still experience a panic attack. It will show itself differently in every person who experiences that. Most of the time crying, rapid heartbeat, and heavy breathing will be the easiest indicators that you are having a panic attack. At the same time, remember to consider other lesser things that might be the actually a panic attack.

Panic attacks and heart attacks have some similar symptoms. So many individuals who are having a panic attack might assume that it's a heart attack. A heart attack causes severe pain within your chest, usually on the left side. You have difficulty breathing, you'll feel lightheaded, and you might sweat or vomit. These things are also very similar within a panic attack. With a panic attack, you won't feel that chest pain as intensely, but it could still be something that is occurring. The biggest difference that you'll notice is that after panic attack, you'll be able to calm down and recover. A heart attack is very severe and could result in death.

Panic attacks aren't going to kill you. Some people might have extreme anxiety to the point that it does lead to a heart attack down the line, but this is not something that you should constantly fear. If you are trembling, shaky, and feeling dizzy or nauseous, these are also signs that you could be having a panic attack. We also have to remember that anxiety is not just being hyperactive and freaking out all the time, You might be extremely lethargic and have a high level of fatigue because of your anxiety. You might feel weak and dizzy, and it can be hard for you to get out of bed in the morning.

These are also issues that can travel into the same symptoms of depression. For both anxiety and depression, you might have consistent random pain throughout your body. If you have constant lower back pain, your first thought might be that there's an issue with your spine or your muscles. In fact, what could the root issue be might simply be depression or anxiety.

The reason that we experience some pain in our muscles is because we are constantly tightening them when we are anxious. Since you have that cortisol release when you're stressed, your muscles tense up a bit. Sometimes, the muscle tension doesn't go away. You will hold that muscle so tightly all throughout the day without even recognizing just how much strain you are putting on our body. It is rather intense, but it's something that we have to remember when trying to evaluate what may be wrong.

At the same time, you could even be more sensitive to pain. We often will experience pain within our jaw line. This can happen because we clench our teeth so tightly throughout the day. You might grind your teeth frequently at night because of our mental sensitivities. This can translate into our body sensitivities too. Something that might not normally hurt you that bad could be the reason that you can't get out of bed.

For example, lower back pain is not great to deal with. However, if you are anxious or depressed, it could be even more intense because your body is more sensitive to the pain. Sometimes people will assume that people who are depressed are being more dramatic when they talk about pain they have, but they really aren't. They're just experiencing pain on a higher level because their body is more sensitive. Your pain tolerance can be lowered when you are depressed. Your shoulders, arms, chest, and abdomen can also be places that you feel a lot of tension. Of course, tension could be anywhere that you have muscles in your body. That means even the tips of your toes could be extremely painful from keeping them clenched all the time. For the most part, you'll feel it within your torso, either the front or the back.

Headaches are also extremely common for people who struggle with anxiety or depression. Depression and anxiety can even be affecting the way that you see the world. Sometimes we look at things and they seem so gray and bleak or more depressed. In reality, it could be impaired vision because of your mental illness. What you have to understand when evaluating these different physical symptoms is their severity. Of course, experiencing certain things is way worse than others. How you will judge your mental illness is based around the extreme way that you might feel it within your body. Don't think that you were being a "baby," or dramatic, or too sensitive when you experience any of these symptoms. They are real physical problems that stem from your mental health. It is not something fabricated or made up. It is a legitimate symptom that needs to be taken care of. When you start to rework your thoughts, that will be the first step in helping you overcome these mental and physical challenges (Leonard, 2018).

Economic Situation

One of the worst things about having so much worry all the time is the way that it affects our financial situation. Financial stress will rule your life. Whether you're somebody who has a ton of money with a high paying job or you have to work 60 hours just to make a couple pennies, you are susceptible to experiencing financial and economic stress. Not only will your specific job cause you to feel these mental pains, but you will also struggle because of the world's economy in general.

We constantly see different news articles and other informative pieces about the state of our economic country at the time. Everybody is always going to make it out to be terrible. How often have you ever seen in history somebody talk about how great the economy was? Even in that moment that it was seemingly better than it is now, people were still worried and stressed. No matter what happens in the world, we are always going to be experiencing monetary stress. It is terrible that it's something that we have to deal with, but in this life, it's not going to go away anytime soon. The way that you experience stress will directly affect your money.

Let's first discover how it will affect your job performance. When you're stressed out, it's going to be a lot harder to work efficiently. You might discover that you are frequently distracted and unable to get tasks done. Even when you went to college, you might have found that you could have performed better, and maybe even gotten a different degree, had you not experienced so much worry over your studies. As you continue to travel throughout your economic life, you may have found that they were opportunities that presented themselves to you, but you weren't able to take them based on your financial standing at the time. Whether you didn't have the money, or you just didn't have the bravery to follow through with a prospective opportunity, there is likely a chance that you missed out on something because of your worry.

Some of us are lucky enough to have jobs that

are intertwined with our passions. This means that work might not be so stressful. At the same time, you might discover that even if you do love your job, you still experience chronic issues with your work life. No matter if you're somebody who loves or hates their job, going to work and having to do this every day can be a very mentally draining task. Work stress can start to seep into your personal life. You might find that it causes you so much anguish that you take it out on your family and friends. We sometimes get so stressed about work because the idea of losing your job might mean that you are very fearful and stressed all the time. We also have to consider the way that stress and anxiety will affect our money habits. If you are somebody who is constantly stressed out then there's a chance that you don't spend your money wisely. You might go shopping or go on constant vacations that you can't afford it all because you're trying to alleviate stress or fulfill a mental anguish within yourself.

You might act impulsively and consistently make purchases that you know you shouldn't. At the same time, those who experienced stress might also be more financially conservative. Maybe you should be spending your money more. Maybe you have a big savings account and you never do anything because you are so stressed about losing your money. Regardless of the financial situation that you are in, the worry you experience will always directly affect your financial situation.

If you have too much money, it might stress you out because you don't know what to do with it and you're afraid of losing it. If you don't have enough money, you might poorly spend what you do have and continually worry about getting more.

Money does keep the world operating in the institutions that we have created. Maybe in a perfect world we could exist without money, but for the time being, it doesn't seem like it's going to go away anytime soon. What we have to recognize is that money is not the answer. Of course, it seems like it will clear you of your stress and your worries right now, and that could be very true. That doesn't mean that it has to necessarily affect your emotional state. It should be an alleviation of worries specified to economics. We have to separate our emotional worries from that and focus on ourselves in our personal life. If you are constantly worried about money, then it is not going to help you make more money. It is just going to cause more stress. To be productive and financially successful, you have to have an emotional control and regulation over yourself so that you can make the right decision and invest or earn properly. Of course, winning the lottery seems like it could take all of your worries away, but remember that if you can't figure out how to be happy in one situation, it will transfer over to the other

Social Skills

Depression and anxiety will directly play into the way that you socially interact within this world. There are some people who are perfectly comfortable with being a very socially friendly person. They might have no issue walking up to strangers and starting a conversation. Perhaps it's introducing themselves that comes with ease. Maybe they love to be the center of attention, and nothing ever stresses them out socially. This is something great, but at the same time, not everybody is able to have these kinds of skills. Worry can cause us to be very socially awkward. We might remove ourselves from situations completely, or when we do find herself within a social setting, it might cause us extreme anxiety.

There are some individuals who will even have diagnosable social anxiety. This is because a chemical imbalance in their brain makes it hard for them to operate in public settings where they must interact with other people. There are a few things that you can understand that could help you better recognize whether or not you have social anxiety.

To start, let's recognize that everybody gets a

little nervous around other people. If you never have been nervous in your life in a social setting, then consider yourself lucky. That's great, and you don't have to worry about this problem. However, many individuals will have specific fear over interacting with other people. You might get nervous before a speech or feel the butterflies in your stomach on a day that you have a date. If this kind of anxiety is debilitating, that is when you know you have a problem. If you are canceling dates, and canceling a speech because of your levels of anxiety, then that is an issue. Having a few flutters is completely normal. It is simply your stress prepping yourself and making sure that you're at the top of your game for whatever you're about to do. If you are constantly feeling dizzy, sick to your stomach, weak, and like you're going to cry just because you have to talk to somebody, then this is a clear sign that there's something wrong.

You might have an extreme fear of being embarrassed or humiliated. The idea that something that could be discovered about you that might cause you shame or guilt, or the idea that somebody is going to cast extreme judgment on you could be something that keeps you from leaving your house. Some people have such bad worry about social settings that they develop agoraphobia, which is the fear of leaving their home. Having poor social skills can really hold you back in life. You might discover it that you don't do the same things that you used to such as going to the gym or interacting within your community. If you're not managing your social anxiety, then it will seep into the rest of your life.

You could discover that you are the type of person who simply cannot be around others. It is a very big struggle, and it's not fun to deal with, but it's something that we have to recognize. What's most important to take away from this section is recognizing that it is completely normal to be slightly fearful of social interaction, but when it interferes with your life, that is when there as a problem. Worry that is constant and rumination after the fact are also indicators that you might have an issue with social anxiety. Recognize how the fear over other people plays into your life. If you don't feel like going to a party simply because you just want to hang out at home, that's fine. That's not social anxiety. If you want to go to a party, but physically can't because you are afraid of what will happen, that is social anxiety. You might discover that you have constant rumination after the fact. This is when you replay situations over and over in your brain or you relive the moments you're with people only focusing on the negative to a point that it makes you sick to your stomach. This is an unhealthy form of reflection that we have to try to work through. We will have some coping mechanisms for the unhealthy thinking patterns that come along with social anxiety in the next chapter, but for now, simply remember that the worry you have will directly affect your social life.

Passion and Motivation

Passion and motivation can be extremely hard to find when we experience constant anxiety or depression. Motivation is something that we all need to have with us to regulate a healthy lifestyle. When you have no motivation, it's going to be hard to want to do anything at all. Passion is also something that can come naturally to us. That should exist inside of all of us. Unfortunately, that's not always the case. Finding the right passion and motivation can be incredibly difficult, especially if you find that you struggle to even get out of bed in the morning.

When you worry, it's usually over something that happened in the past or fear over the future. To be passionate and motivated, then you do have to consider everything that you might go through in the future. Having motivation is all about building a better tomorrow. Unfortunately, when you do experience something like anxiety, you're not thinking about tomorrow in a productive way. Instead, you're only considering the things that might go bad. You're only thinking about all the terrible and worst case scenarios when you are experiencing anxiety or depression.

To make sure that we better enable ourselves to be happier, motivated, and passionate, there are few things that we can do to create this within ourselves. The first thing you'll have to do is come face to face with is why you are so lacking motivation. Sometimes it can be as simple as not focusing on the right goals. Everybody has different wishes and desires in their life and there are some people who will only attach themselves to the goals and desires that other people have. If you legitimately want to increase your life and live happier, then it's time to consider if your goals are things that you want for yourself. For example, there is a big pressure on people in the world to go through the motions of going to college, getting a great job, finding a spouse, buying a house, getting a car, adopting a pet, and having X number of children. This is a normal goal, and it's perfectly fine if you legitimately want that. Unfortunately, a lot of people don't. Some individuals are happier pursuing a career. Maybe they want to just have children, but they don't care about the rest of the stuff. Others might simply want to get married but not have to have any children. Everybody's goals are different, so you have to confront yourself and question if these goals are things that you actually want for yourself.

Aside from that, we have to recognize if the things that we are doing in our life actually align with those goals. For example, if your dream is to study, pursue knowledge and explore the world, but you have been working at the same desk job that barely pays for the past five years, you are not doing anything for those goals. You might have a clear idea for what you desire in your life, but the activities that you're doing, are not helping you fulfill those dreams. One method of helping you consider if you are doing the right thing is to make a list of all of your goals and dreams.

Write out at least 20 things. Then on a separate sheet of paper, write out everything that you do on a daily basis. What activities are normal for you? For example, your top five goals might be to:

- travel the world
- buy a house
- adopt a dog
- have a baby
- make $500,000.

These are just random goals that anybody could have, and they're all great.

Then actually make your list of things that you do. The top things might be:

- go to work at the bank from nine to

five every day

- go grocery shopping and cook different meals

- re-watch old episodes of your favorite show

- go to bars and party on the weekend

- spend time at the dog park

As your listing things out, do you see how even though you know those goals so clearly, the things that are actually being done don't align with those goals? The reason that you might lack motivation and passion for that list of tasks is because it doesn't matter to you. You don't care about doing any of those things. Going to the bar is just a distraction. Re-watching old reruns is just a habit, and so on. Of course, going into a bar and watching old TV shows is great. That's a fun thing to do and if that's what you want to do, by all means do that. We are simply talking about how the goals don't really align with the actual activities, and this is why there might be a lack of motivation. That disconnect occurs and so the passion dies in the process.

We can't always achieve all of our goals, of course. However, you can still find a way that the tasks you do every day play into those goals so that you can find that motivation. For example, working that desk job could mean that you are saving money to invest to make that $500K. Skipping out on the bar means that you are saving money so that you can save for travel to see the world. While they might not exactly match each other, you can still discover methods of including your tasks and your goals so they can work together.

It's going to take a while to reach your goals, and you might not even fully discover what they are yet. Simply, remember that because of this, you might be struggling with finding passion and motivation within yourself because of the constant worry that you have.

Sleep Habits and Stress

Worry and sleep go together like peanut butter and hot sauce. They're two very common things, but when you mix it together, it's a horrible combination. When you are stressed, you won't be able to sleep as easily. When you can't get the right amount of sleep, it will cause even more stress. It is a toxic and vicious cycle that as incredibly challenging to deal with. Nobody should have to always worry about not getting enough sleep.

You might discover that you stay up all night because you're constantly thinking about things that worry you. Even if you do fall asleep, you might have night terrors and other horrible dreams that cause you to wake up or not get the restful sleep that you deserve. If you are tired throughout your day, then you won't be able to function as well as you could if you were rested. Therefore, you'll end up experiencing even more stress. There are a few things that we can do to make sure that we reduce our stress so we can get a good night's sleep.

The first thing that you have to consider is the time that you are going to bed. We all know that we need to go to bed sooner. There's no doubt about that. What we don't consider is that laying down in bed does not indicate the time that we fall asleep. You have to give yourself an hour to wind down. Schedule a time where you can worry and ruminate rather than just hoping that you don't. If you have to go to bed by midnight every night to get your proper seven hours of sleep, then make sure that you are in bed by 11 p.m. You could still sit there and read a book or maybe even watch something on TV. It is preferred that you keep the screens away from you because the blue light that comes off will affect your sleep. At the same time, just simply make sure that you can wind down before going to bed and expecting to fall asleep.

Another thing you can do is make sure that you keep your phone across the room from you. There are a few reasons for this. The first reason is so that you aren't tempted to pull your phone out. Sometimes when you struggle to fall asleep, the first thing you do is to reach for your phone to distract yourself. You can get caught on internet frenzy and spend two hours scrolling the web instead of actually falling asleep.

The second reason is because we might find that it is easy to set multiple alarms and then consistently hit the snooze to ignore them. You might be the type of person to have to wake up at 7:30, that means you set your first alarm for 6:55, and another at seven, then another at 7:05, then another at 7:10, and so on. While It is good to make sure that you wake up at the right time, all you are doing is prolonging an unhealthy sleeping habits. Sleep is something that needs to be peaceful and deep.

That surface level sleep where we're just kind of dozing off is not healthy. It is not going to help you be more energized throughout your day. If you have to wake up at 7:30, then wake up at 7:30. Set your phone across your room. If you have a bathroom connected to your room, put your phone somewhere in there. That way, by the time you stand up, walk to your phone, and turn the alarm off, you'll be in the bathroom already and more likely to stay awake. That way, you'll probably have to use the toilet right away so you'll use it, open your phone, check your email, and by the time you do all that you will be fully awake. This is a much healthier way to wake up instead of having a phone next to us that we keep snoozing every five minutes over and over again. That's just starting your day off terrible, and it's going to put you in a bad mood. It is incredibly difficult to get out of bed in the morning, especially if you experience anxiety and depression, but you're only prolonging that experience when you set those multiple alarms rather than just getting up out of bed the first time.

There are other simple things you can do like making sure that you limit your caffeine and sugar intake before bag and trying some meditative practices. Whatever you do, always start by calming your mind before you fall asleep at night.

DISTINGUISHING BETWEEN REAL AND IMAGINARY FEARS

When you were a child, were you ever afraid that there was a monster hiding under your bed or in your closet? Perhaps you cried until a parent came in and showed you that there was nothing to be afraid of. Even though that fear was imaginary the symptoms that you felt are not fake. When we are confronted with problems that don't exist, we can still feel all the terrible stress and worry that comes along with that. It is incredibly frustrating to be so afraid of something that seems so small. Perhaps you are the type of person who struggles to confront people in public. Maybe they got your coffee order wrong, and instead of saying something you just drink the coffee, even though it's disgusting. Maybe somebody got your name wrong, and they continue to call you by the wrong name. Instead of telling them, you just go by this name that isn't even yours all because you're afraid of what will happen when you tell the truth.

There are many real fears that we have in life, and common things that scare us that are socially acceptable. We also have many fears in life that are completely not real and that we don't have to worry about. Unfortunately, telling somebody to just "not worry," or that "it's not a big deal," is not going to solve the problem. What you have to do is ensure that you look at the root of your issues and determine whether they are real or imaginary.

A cognitive distortion is an unhealthy pattern of thinking that will keep you in a place where you are constantly having negative thoughts. First, we're going to break down your fears into standard biological reactions. These are the core fears that we have as humans. These are common things that scare us that we have recognized among many different individuals. After we discuss this, we will go into what different cognitive distortions are, as well as a few tips for reversing that thought process.

Standardized Biological Reaction

Imagine a large oak tree towering above you. As you get closer you see the insane intricate designs of the smaller branches and leaves blowing through the wind. Each of these branches has so many leaves but help create the bushy appearance of the tree. If you look at one leaf, then it'll connect back to a smaller twig, which attaches itself to a branch, which attaches to a bigger branch, and so on. If you look at all of these leaves, each one goes back to the tree trunk. This is the base which manufactures the rest of the leaves in the surrounding organism.

You could have hundreds of leaves, but they might all come from the same five trees. That is how we need to recognize our fear. Fear is a normal response to a stimulant. It is the recognition that there is knowledge that needs to be processed, or a situation which demands a decision. When it comes to recognizing these different kinds of fears, we can look at each one and trace it back to **five** different types of fears. These are referred to as your standard biological reactions. The thing about fear is that no matter what it is that caused you fear, your body will generally react in the same way. How each of us interacts with our fears on an individual level will be different. For example, you might clam up and close yourself off whenever you're scared. You might have a friend who gets more aggressive and readier to throw fists when they get upset.

The thing is, when we experience fear individually, we react to it in the same way. You might react by clamming up and getting scared. Your friend who is more willing to throw a punch. If a spider dropped onto your head and started crawling on your body, you might be a little bit more inclined to be silently freaked out and brush it off. The friend who throws punches is going to freak out, stand up, yell, scream, and so on. If you find out that you are getting fired from your job, then you might be more passive, calm, and collected in that way. Then the friend who throws punches would react to getting fired by being aggressive and angry. The situation that presents itself to us will elicit a similar reaction in the individual, regardless of how they specifically react compared to their peers. When we understand these basic core fears, we have to recognize that they all will produce and manufacture different fears within that.

The most important thing to consider out of everything else is that no matter what you are scared of, you can trace it back to something bigger. It is a greater biological instinct that we have that we can be afraid of experiencing, which is why we might react a certain way to fear. Let's go through those five now. They are:

- extinction
- mutilation
- loss of autonomy
- separation
- ego death.

These are the five basic fears, and no matter what happens or what emotions you experience, you can likely trace that feeling back to one of these five fears. Let's first start with extinction. This is obvious. There's something inside of us that tells us we need to stay alive. Even when people are feeling depressed and suicidal, they don't always go through with it because something inside of them still keeps them here. Even if you don't have outside sources like money, a great family, friends, and other things to live for, then, you still have this biological urge within you that tells you to keep living. Even when you might get attacked, beat up, or are suffering an intense painful illness, your body will continue to fight. Very rarely will an animal, whether it's human or not, lay down and simply take the torture.

We just have this urge to continue to live.

Extinction is total annihilation. It is the fear that we have of death.

This extinction factor will show itself in many different ways. In one instance, you might be afraid of going on an airplane. This can simply be because you're afraid that the airplane will crash and you will die. Then, there are some individuals who are afraid of aging. They might do everything they can to look younger and have a youthful appearance because it makes them feel younger. We get afraid of aging because that means we're getting closer to death. That is extinction in itself.

This extinction feeling is felt when you are driving in a fast car with somebody and you're afraid of a car accident. It is what you get when you are walking along a high building, and you feel like you might fall off. It is what you feel when you have pain in your body and you're worried that you have cancer that you're dying because something in you hurts. This extinction fear will manifest itself in many different ways, but it is one of the five core basic fears we have.

Moving on to the next is mutilation. This is the fear of losing a part of ourselves. Whether it's physical or mental, we have this fear that we are going to have a part of our bodies mutilated.

For example, if you're boiling hot water, you're not going to stick your hand in the water because you're afraid of losing your hand. You know that by sticking your hand in the water you wouldn't die, but you would probably burn your hand, potentially to the point that you couldn't even use your hand anymore. We also fear losing part of our mental abilities. You might have a high level of integrity or pride. You don't want to embarrass yourself because you don't want to lose that dignity. This is a common fear that we have. You have to look at your own life and determine how it might manifest itself but remember that fear of simply losing part of you is a very normal and very common as to be expected among various individuals.

The third fear that we have is our loss of autonomy. Your autonomy is like your freedom. It is your ability to make choices for yourself and discover the best possible decisions or solutions for your life. We have this loss of autonomy fear because we don't want that freedom taken away from us. We need to be able to make our own decisions and have that freedom within our life. This is, again, is in a mental or a physical way. This is why some people will have the fear of getting trapped in an elevator. It reminds them of imprisonment and makes you feel caged or confined so that kind of restriction can really cause fear. We also can feel that when we might be controlled by other people. If you have a controlling parent or spouse in your life, then it probably causes you worry. This is because you are putting yourself in their hands, and they are having control over you. There are plenty of times when we want to be controlled by other people. Sometimes it's nice to be given a task to do. Maybe you're at work and you don't have anything to fill your time and your boss gives you a few things to finish during the day. That kind of control is not something that limits our freedom; it just puts a few restrictions or some structure to our autonomy that exists already. When you have somebody that is telling you what to do and not giving you an option of whether you can do it, that is when we feel as though our autonomy is restricted.

Again, look at your own life and discover the way that this fear might be causing worry. Do you have physical restrictions that make you worried?

Perhaps your apartment is incredibly small and cramped. This could be enough to just make you feel like you are in a prison. Even having depression alone can make us feel like we are in a mental cage. That smothered feeling can cause you to be paralyzed, therefore, leading to even more worry about your autonomy.

Moving on, we have a fourth fear which is abandonment. This is separation. This is rejection. This is when you are an outcast and not validated by other people. As we already mentioned, we are a group species so we do depend on other people to help build that esteem within us.

When we don't have that, then it makes us feel as though we might be alone. If you struggle in your life with control issues, then there's a really good chance you are afraid of abandonment. If you were left by a parent at a young age, or if you did have parents who neglected you, then they didn't play an active role in your life or building that esteem. In turn, you might discover that you lack the ability to have confidence within yourself because that was never taught to you as a child. What can happen as a result is that now you try to control the situation. If you feel as though you don't have any control over your life, then you will look for that power in other places.

This fear of abandonment is something that makes us feel not wanted. If you have worries over your esteem and you lack confidence, then this is probably at the core.

Finally, the fifth fear is your ego death. This is when you might experience shame or embarrassment. If you ever experienced a time when you're humiliated and you feel like you may have lost a part of yourself, then this is also a fear. It kind of plays into a mixture of all of these if you really look at it but, in general, this is just the fear that we might end up losing part of our personality.

When we talk about egos, people think that we mean egotistical. They imagine somebody with a big head walking around like they're a hot shot. That's not the case. Your ego is a lot more complex than that.

Your ego is your self-importance. It is how you view yourself and, in turn, that can translate into how other people view you. As we discussed, everybody has a certain esteem they need to satisfy, and if that's not being fulfilled, then it will destroy your esteem. This is why many individuals will struggle with how they look and their confidence levels. It is not just about being embarrassed by how you look physically. Sometimes, it's what you say. You might feel constant embarrassment or shame over silly jokes or small comments that you make when talking to other people. This translates back into that fear of the ego death.

Now that you understand these five core fears, what does that mean for your level of worry?

Well, whenever you do find yourself constantly experiencing that same kind of feeling over and over again, you can look at the root. As we discussed, it's only once you go to the deepest root and pluck that out that the weed will stop growing back. Figure out the patterns of thinking that cause you to consistently have these fears, and you will begin to know how to treat that. Let's now move on to some cognitive distortions. Cognitive distortion is a pattern of thinking that leaves you trapped in a toxic mental cycle.

Now that you understand these five core fears, what does that mean for your level of work? The common cognitive distortions are the ones that we are going to discuss below, but there are many different types of CDs that can cause mental ailments (Albrecht, 2012).

Polarized Thinking

The first cognitive distortion that we're going to discuss is polarized thinking. What this is inclusive of is creating a spectrum for which you begin to judge everything. A spectrum is when there is one side and then the other side. For example, hot versus cold is on a spectrum. Cold, or freezing, is on one end and then boiling hot is on the other. Everything that you find would fall within a category of whether it is freezing cold or boiling hot. Some things will be right in the center and that's what we often refer to as room temperature. Some things are going to be a little bit cold, but not very cold. Some things will be warm, but not hot. Everything will fall in place within that spectrum.

Polarized thinking is when we start this mentality that everything has to fall on either one side of the spectrum or the other. We begin to believe that everything is either black or white. We don't allow our thoughts to fall into that complex gray area in between. What ends up happening is that we label everything as either good or bad. It is easy to label anything is good or bad if you really think about it. Of course, things like murder, rape, or kidnapping and the most horrible crimes you could ever think are pretty much 100% bad. You can't really find the good in those scenarios. However, other things could be good or bad. Even getting fired from your job could be good.

It could be a kickstart into a new life. Maybe you get fired from a job you've been working at for 10 years and discover you didn't like that job. You move on and you find an even greater position. Being broken sounds pretty bad, but maybe you discover that it was actually good for you because then you move on and find a relationship that's even better.

As you can see, many things will have different perspectives. Even something like a person dying in a car accident is absolutely horrible and no family should ever have to deal with that. However, they might end up donating an organ, such as their heart or a kidney to somebody who would die without that organ. For that family of the patient who gets to live, that's a great thing.

It's not like they're celebrating a party about this person dying, but we can still acknowledge that even in the most horrific, unthinkable, and unimaginable situations, something good could be there.

Black and white thinking is the label that it has to be good or bad. That's where things get tricky. That's where you would label that car accident as bad or you would label it as good. That's not true. It is good and bad. It might lean more toward bad, but it still isn't all the way to the left or right necessarily. It is probably more on the bad side, since it is unexpected for that family and the other family had already somewhat prepared for the illness of that patient. There's also always the chance that they could have gotten that organ from another individual. Of course, what we all want is everybody to live and be happy, but in this world we know that that isn't the case.

When we only think of things in black and white, it really limits your thought process. Black and white is the cognitive distortion that just keeps you trapped on one spectrum or the other. When you label everything as either good or bad, then you do the same thing to your entire life. You will label your life as bad, you label the world as a bad, and you label people as a bad. If you look for it, there could be more bad than good in the world. At the same time, if you look for it, there could be more good than bad in the world. We shouldn't be continually comparing things on such a strict scale like this. When you do, that's what creates those polarized thoughts.

To combat this, start to look at the opposite end of the spectrum. This doesn't mean that you have to believe it either. So many people are turned away from the other side of their polarized thoughts. It is not that they can't recognize them, it's that they refuse to think about them. Imagine that you are having a heated debate with somebody about something the two of you completely disagree on. Maybe it's a TV show. You think it's the best TV show ever made, and they think it's complete garbage.

You disagree with them and you don't believe them. But can't you see their point? Can you at least try to hear them out and understand what they're saying? The problem with black and white thinking is that people get so stuck at one end of the spectrum, they forget that the other side is even there.

Of course, it's not your job to identify the good in everything. Sometimes things just aren't great. They'll just be bad and you'll just have a terrible day. That's fine, but a terrible day doesn't mean that you have a terrible life. Getting a ticket on your car doesn't mean that you have to have a terrible day the rest of the time. Ordering a hot sandwich and finding out that it's cold doesn't mean that your day is in total ruins. Spilling coffee on your shirt doesn't mean that you are a bad person.

Even losing a loved one doesn't mean that your life has to end. Of course, that's a terrible thing and you are allowed to grieve for as long as you need. But to let instance ruin an entire existence is not healthy.

It's okay to see the bad. It is okay to not want to feel what's good. That doesn't mean that we can't acknowledge it. There will always be the other side of the coin. There will always be a silver lining. You have to figure out what that gray area is. Not everything needs to be labeled as good or bad. Not everything will be labeled as being in the direct middle either.

A common example of this would be taking a

small trait of somebody and letting that define them as a person. For example, maybe you meet somebody who is really obsessed with a particular musician who you think is totally awful. Maybe they like to go to their concerts and hang out with them and listen to their music.

You might absolutely hate this artist and that's fine. The two of you do not have to like the same music. At the same time if you let that define them as who they are, then you could be missing out on a lot of other great things. Maybe they recognize that the artist isn't really that great, but they could have a nostalgic connection to this person that dates back to their teen years, maybe they appreciate the art style of the music, or they just have something else that makes them like it. Just because we like certain things doesn't mean that has to define us. Don't let polarized thinking trick you into believing this is true.

Personalization

Personalization is the next cognitive distortion that will be discussing. What this involves is when the individual believes that everybody is out to get them. They will assume that the chatter they hear or the snickering, they overheard is all something that directly involves them. Personalization is when you will put yourself at the center of everybody else's issues. The problem with this is that we disregard the fact that other people are in control of their own emotions. An example of personalization would start with an insecure person. This individual might have a very low self-esteem and have almost no confidence.

They're walking down the street one day and they overhear a few people chatter and laugh. As they're walking away from this group of people, they assume that those individuals are laughing at them. They let this sour their day. Later on, that same individual goes to a party. They're having a decent time and then they get talking to a group of people. They make a joke, and only a few people laugh, and some others don't seem like they thought it was that funny. It wasn't an offensive joke, it just wasn't that original.

This individual goes home and feels terrible. They constantly ruminate over that. They worry about what other people thought and they let this ruin the rest of their week. They think about it day after day, constantly going over and over in their brain. Personalization is a toxic mentality that keeps us trapped in a cycle of worrying.

Even if that joke was embarrassing at the party, then they need to understand that they're not in control of other people's emotions. By assuming that they ruined the party, they take power over other people's emotions, and that's not fair. By jumping to the conclusion that that group of people were chattering and laughing at them, they are assuming that those people were even thinking of them in the first place. This is where our ego gets a little out of control. It is not that we're egotistical and we think we're better than everybody, it's simply that we only see our own perspective. We're only looking at our version of the story.

You might have even made a terrible an embarrassing joke that did offend somebody. To still assume that it ruined an entire party is a stretch. This is personalization.

To remove yourself from this pattern of thinking, recognize that other people are in charge of their emotions. Even if you did manage to offend somebody and ruin the party, it was still their decision to have that reaction. Of course, we can influence other people's emotions and we could do things that trigger certain feelings, but you never plant a thought in somebody else's head. Unless you were actively brainwashing, you aren't responsible for the way that a person thinks. We can't assume that responsibility because that's a heavy weight on our shoulders. That is going to constantly cause stress and anxiety.

To avoid personalization, ensure that you recognize you are only in control of your own thoughts and feelings. Even if the worst-case scenario does happen with other people, than that is still out of your control. It is their responsibility to work through their own thoughts and feelings.

Blaming

Another cognitive distortion is always blaming. It is so easy to blame somebody else. It was the car in front of yours fault that you were late for work. It was your friend's fault that you were in a bad mood because she texted you something annoying. It is your mom's fault now that you're an alcoholic because she was an alcoholic first. You could blame every problem you have on other people. This is something that you could totally choose to do, however, it is a cognitive distortion, and it will cause worry in your life.

You will have an unhappy and dismal existence if you only know how to blame other people. You are completely valid in wanting to put blame on other people, and you are totally justified for acknowledging somebody else's influence over your life. At the same time, the moment that you start to blame somebody else is when you give them control over your life.

If you really want to have power over your thoughts and emotions, you have to accept responsibility for them. That does not mean that you accept responsibility for what happened to you. You are simply choosing to not place your emotional state within the hands of other people anymore.

On the opposite end, you might also blame yourself. Let's say you went to an outing with some friends at an event. The friends that you met up with all seem a little bit anxious or sad at the end. Perhaps a few things went wrong, and everyone just had a mediocre time. You might go home and blame yourself for that.

Again, by doing this you're accepting the responsibility of other people's emotions. Even if it's something insanely out of your control, you might blame yourself. For example, if you forget to recycle a plastic cup, maybe you sit there for hours and agonize and blame yourself for the environmental damage that currently exists. Of course, we all play an individual role in the state of our ecosystem. At the same time, one plastic cup does not cause environmental damage.

By taking such great blame, you're putting all of those emotions on yourself, and that is toxic. Another form of blaming that kind of plays into the same cognitive distortion is assuming that you always have to be right. Again, this is when we take on emotions that are our responsibility by assuming that you are always right, you are forgetting the other person and how they might be involved. It is great to think that you're an intelligent and smart individual; we all should be very proud of our knowledge. However, you can't assume that you are always right. A truly intelligent individual understands that the more they know, the more they have yet to learn.

To make sure that you are not blaming other people, look at your own role within the situation. Now, if you are somebody whose entire family was murdered by a random serial killer, obviously, you're going to put the blame on them. That's totally fine. That is one of the rare instances where you can't really accept any responsibility for that situation.

Not everything is so extreme in this way. Most individuals simply blame others because they don't have enough money, or because they're sick, or because they're unhealthy or because they're unhappy. We can't do this. We have to accept *some* responsibility in our life. It is not taking blame, and it's not putting the fault on anybody. It is simply recognizing that our emotional state is within *our* control. We have to do what we can to work through that in a healthy way.

Overgeneralization

The fourth cognitive distortion that we're going to discuss is overgeneralization. This is when we make assumptions. It is using absolutes and jumping to conclusions. An absolute is a word that defines an entire situation. This involves words like:

- always/never
- should have/could have
- can't/won't
- best/worst
- definitely
- nothing/everything

These absolute phrases lead to overgeneralization. When you have a cognitive distortion that involves overgeneralization, this is when you take one single instance and you twist it so that is the whole defining the solution to the scenario. For example, think back on all the little annoying things we discussed earlier.

If you get a parking ticket, that is annoying to deal with. Nobody wants to have to go through that. However, if you take that parking ticket and let it define the rest of your day and you have a bad day because of it, that's overgeneralization. You might go home and tell a friend that you got a parking ticket, so your day was awful. When you do that, you ignore everything else that happened between. You take that one emotion and you let that ruin the entire day that you have when you jump to conclusions. You're also jumping over everything else in between that could make the situation have more sense.

For example, let's say that you invited a bunch of people to a party. You only end up hearing back from half the people you invited, and only about half of them show up to the party. You can instantly jump to the conclusion that nobody likes you and everybody's out to get you. This is a very common thought process we have especially after experiencing some forms of rejection. When you jump to that conclusion you miss out all the minor little details in between. You forgot the fact that you waited until two days before to invite people. You didn't consider that it was the beginning of June, so many people are going to be going to graduation parties. You forgot the fact that you already knew that three of your friends were out of town.

When you jump to that conclusion you ignore reality and instead you only validate the negative perspective that already exist within yourself.

When you over generalize too much, it can leave into another cognitive distortion, known as catastrophizing. What this means is that you are always expecting the worst possible thing to happen. You assume that just because you're going to go through an experience that might have a negative outcome, that this is what will be involved. Again, to touch on the plane analogy, you might be afraid to fly because you assume that the plane is going to crash.

This is overgeneralization and jumping to conclusions. Yes, it is possible for an airplane to crash. Does this happen frequently? No. It is not fair for us to assume that it's going to happen the one time that we ride a plane. That's overgeneralization. If it were to happen, then that is a complete coincidence and just a random freak accident. It is not something that we could have ever predicted or assumed, so we can't live our lives pretending as though that is possible (Grohol, 2019).

PROCRASTINATION INTO PRODUCTIVITY

Sometimes, the reason why you might struggle to get a task done is because you are so worried about whether you're going to get it done. Procrastination is a terribly uncomfortable thing to have to deal with. It causes us so much anxiety because we are constantly afraid of what might happen once we complete a task.

What you might not know about procrastination is that it can actually be a form of anxiety. Some people think procrastinating is simply because they are lazy. That is not true at all. In fact, procrastination can happen to some of the strongest willed and motivated people. We get afraid of the things that might happen once we complete the task.

Sometimes not doing something at all is better than dealing with what might happen if we failed at that task. Of course, this is not how we should be living our life, but it is how many people have formed a mentality around completing a task. In this chapter, we're going to help you recognize bad habits, replace them with a good clear mind, and then develop positive thoughts to help you overcome procrastination. In the end, you'll be able to find productivity and motivation within yourself. This is an incredibly powerful tool that will keep you strong and independent throughout each venture you choose to take.

Recognizing Bad Habits and Replacing Them With Good

It can be incredibly challenging to recognize bad habits because we don't even always understand that they there. When you've been experiencing a certain type of behavior and going through the same motions over and over again your entire life, then it's going to be a huge struggle to actually pick out and identify the toxic behaviors that you might have been exhibiting.

There are many bad habits that we fall into that can consistently set us back in life. If you really want to improve on yourself and discover all the things that you've been hoping for, then it's time to start picking out our bad habits. Let's first acknowledge a few bad habits that are common, and then we will go ahead and discuss what you can do to replace that bad habit.

The first habit that many individuals find themselves in is simply dealing with the situation and hoping that it gets better. How many times have you had a problem at work, and you thought to yourself that this was the last straw? Maybe you went home and fluffed up your resume in the hopes that by doing this you would eventually be able to discover a more lucrative position. It is certainly something that would be feasible, but you decide later that you'd rather just hang around and deal with the problem. Instead of continuing to push on and work through to resolve your issues, you just simply become complacent and let this bad thing happen. You just "hope for the best."

Sometimes, it's easier to just stay quiet and deal with it than it would be to actually work through your emotions in a healthy and normal way. Another bad habit that many people might discover is that they hang out with people who don't appreciate them. You might discover that people treat you negatively, and you simply allow this to happen. Sometimes we let it happen because we legitimately believe we aren't good people that don't deserve love or happiness.

Other times, we let it happen because again, it's easier to just be passive and not say anything than to continue to try to confront them or change them.

Another bad habit that you might have is that you procrastinate and that you're always late. Time management seems like an issue with our tasks and the actual time period we're given. In reality, time management has to deal a lot with your mentality and the effort that you might put into certain things. If you're not fully invested in a task or project, then that will show through the way that you prioritize it with your time.

Once you are able to start recognizing some of your bad habits, then it's time to replace them. Of course, you probably have some bad habits on your own that weren't mentioned, and you will definitely need to do some self-reflection to figure out what these are. Don't just think of bad habits as things like smoking, drinking, eating junk food, not exercising, biting your nails, and so on. Of course, those are bad habits that you should do your best to get out of, but what we're really referring to is your ability to recognize these mental patterns and break them.

We're not just talking about things that you do physically for your body that you need to change, we're mostly emphasizing the mental patterns and cognitive distortions to pull yourself out of.

The first thing you can do to break these bad habits is to always challenge your thoughts. Each time you think "It doesn't matter," "I'm not that great," "I don't deserve better," or so on, challenge that thought. Ask yourself where it came from. Who put the idea in your head that it's okay for you to be complacent in a relationship that doesn't bring you any joy or happiness? Where did you get the idea that you deserve to deal with a negative workspace?

Always question the root of where these beliefs come from, and you will be able to create the intellectual mind needed to avoid falling back into another unhealthy pattern. The best way to break a habit is to replace it with a new one. This means that each time that you do identify a negative thought, try to establish a positive one that could take its place. If you look in the mirror and think to yourself that you are an ugly, hideous monster, what can you use to replace that thought with instead? You can boost yourself up by reminding you that you are an individual and inspirational, beautiful person. To avoid bad habits, there are a few other things that we can do. You can also make sure to avoid or confront the triggers that you have. For example, if a bad habit were binge eating junk food, then the trigger would be keeping ice cream in the freezer. This would obviously trigger you to want to eat that ice cream later. To ensure that you are breaking that habit, remove that trigger.

If you notice that you consistently let negative people into your life, discover what that trigger is. Is it that your self-esteem is that low and requires you to surround yourself with individuals who will boost your ego? If this is the case, then you can recognize that it's probably time to let these people go and avoid them as you start to heal yourself. If you're struggling to really break these bad habits, that it might be time for you to get the help of somebody else.

By using an outside source like a friend or a relative, they can hold you accountable for your behavior. You can help them to understand what your bad habit might be, and they can work through those issues with you. For example, if you are a very negative thinker that always comes home and discusses how terrible your day is, let your roommate know that this is a habit you're trying to break. When you come home and start to vent to them, they can say to you to stop and to revert that behavior so that it's no longer a toxic pattern.

The best way to start new habits is to make a big change. Whether it's something as big as quitting your job and moving to a new state or simply rearranging the furniture in your living room, you have to change something in order to elicit a new life.

You can't expect to heal within the same boundaries that the worry was created in the first place.

Clearing Your Mind and Developing Positive Thoughts

When you have a closet or a drawer full of

clutter, there's a good chance that you know how much worry this can cause. Each time you pass that physical clutter, it might give you anxiety. Your mental clutter can cause just as much anguish.

There are few steps that you can do to clear your mind for more positive and healthy thinking. The first thing to do is to establish a place that doesn't have any physical clutter. When you see that physical clutter, your mind still has to register it. Even though you're not actively thinking to yourself about the stack of magazines in the corner of the room, your mind glosses over that as you scan the area you are in, and something in your brain will still trigger a thought response. You might not consciously think about it, but it will subconsciously build in the back of your head. This is why, even if you don't really care about clean space, consciously being in a dirty space over and over again will consistently clutter your brain. It is best to keep a clean and organized environment. This doesn't mean that you have to be a minimalist who throws everything away. If you keep it organized, then that kind of structure will replicate itself within your brain, and you won't struggle with having so much mental fog all of the time when you can really have a relaxed and clear head. It'll be easier to confront your worries. You will have the power to recognize the things that you struggle with, and you'll be able to work through that in a healthy and productive manner.

Another thing that will help you really clear up your mental space is to keep track of your thoughts, physically. This means that you can start to mentally think about certain things that you want to learn and write it down. You can also keep track of your thoughts with a journal by taking notes. The first thing that you're doing is validating your thoughts. After you've done this sort of validation, then you can move on, and reflect on those thoughts. You can keep track of mental habits too. You can write down your feelings every day for a month. Then at the end of the 30 days look back to see if there's a greater truth about yourself that you could pull from this.

Finally, another way that we can help you decrease some of your mental clutter is to stop multitasking. Multitasking seems like the most efficient way to get things done. Really, it just creates more tasks within your head. It makes you believe that you have less time than you do, and it puts the pressure on you to complete things quicker. When you multitask, you're giving 50% or 30% to everything you do, when you can simply do the task to give it 100%. In the end, it would probably each take the same amount of time. It just feels like you're doing more since you're doing multiple things at once. Dedicate yourself 100% to each thing you do, and you'll find that it actually takes less time than if you try to split things up.

Once you have that clear head, it'll be a lot easier to start to develop more positive thoughts. Being positive is not easy. Our brain tends to pick out the bad, perhaps as a survival tactic or maybe just something that we've been conditioned to believe. When you look at the bad of something, then you improve it, rather than just looking at the good and celebrating it. Improving is great but if we only look at the bad all the time, it will create a negative mindset.

There are a few things you can do to increase your positive thinking.

The first thing is to practice gratitude. What this means is recognizing your gratefulness and thankfulness for a situation. Rather than looking at the bad you shift your focus to the good. Instead of wishing for things that you don't have you recognize how to appreciate what already exists within your life. It is not easy, but it is something that can really change the way that you think.

Another way to positively think is to accept failure. Often, we get so afraid of what might happen if we don't succeed that it paralyzes us and keeps us from actually successfully completing a task. When it comes to positive thinking, accept that failure is going to be part of the journey. Everybody who has ever succeeded at something is a person who failed, but decided to try again.

Life is not a lottery. We can't just hope that one day we'll be good at something. We can't just expect that tomorrow will be able to be an expert. You have to practice and that means failing and improving. Each time you go through something challenging, it just means that you're going to be stronger in the end.

These methods are all ways you can start to think more positively.

Overcoming Procrastination

Procrastination is an ugly monster that exists in our life. No longer do you have to be trapped within a procrastinating mindset.

There are a few steps that you can take. We already discussed why you might procrastinate, and we already discussed what procrastination even looks like. Sometimes we procrastinate because finishing it means that we're going to get feedback. For example, if you procrastinate writing a paper for school for a month, then you are probably doing this because you are afraid of what they are going to say about your paper once you've turned it in. By not doing something, then we can avoid the pain that might come if we fail. This is one of the reasons why people might procrastinate.

You have to look deep within yourself and ask on an individual level what it is that is keeping you from completing the task. After that there are a few things you can do to stop procrastination. The first thing you can do is to forgive yourself get over the fact that you've waited so long already.

Let's say that you have a test on Monday, and you knew about it since Thursday. You could have started studying on Thursday, but instead you waited until Sunday night at 10 p.m. You finally have some of that motivation, but you can't get over the fact that you should have done it sooner. You might keep thinking that to yourself over and over again and questioning why you just didn't do this on Thursday. Forgive yourself for waiting so long and accept the fact that you can't go back in time. It is better to just do something now than to add more time on top of what you already spent procrastinating.

Just start to do something. We always get overwhelmed by our work because our project or our papers or whatever else we're procrastinating on might be sitting right in front of us. It feels so overwhelming to have to complete a 20-page paper. Break it down into smaller bits. Tell yourself that as long as you do one page, that is better than doing nothing at all. Give yourself the smallest possible task. After you complete one page, you'll realize that it really wasn't that bad at all. Starting is always the hard part. Once you get the ball rolling, it's going to keep spinning without you even having to try. Open your computer and look at your paper. That's the first step. After that, write the first page. That's it. If that's all you could really do in a day, then congratulate yourself because that's better than doing nothing at all. What you'll usually discover is that after you do that first page, it's easier to do the second and the third and the fourth, and so on, until you finished. Rarely do we procrastinate things that are almost done. Most of the time procrastination happens before we even got started.

Of course, do normal practical things to help you focus better, like removing your distractions, listening to relaxing or classical music, making sure that you're not hungry or tired, and so on. These are practical things that we have to consider, but the truth about procrastination is that it exists within your mind, and that is the root from what you have to solve the problem.

CONTROLLING YOUR EMOTIONS AND IMPROVING RELATIONSHIPS

Worry and anxiety can cause a lot of issues within your personal relationships. Whether you constantly fight with other people or you are afraid to stand up for something that is bothering you, when we don't control our emotions, it means that we can't control our relationships.

One thing that you have to remember before getting into the meat of this chapter is that you can't control other people. No matter how hard you might want to try to change somebody's mood or make them see something so obvious, it's not your responsibility to do this at the end of the day. Of course, you should be doing your best to have a healthy relationship where you can communicate openly with others. But at the same time, if somebody isn't willing to change, sometimes you just have to focus on yourself. This can be challenging, but what's most important is that you make sure to look out for yourself first.

There's a powerful metaphor that is often used in mental health that can help us describe the way that we need to take care of ourselves first.

If you were to ride an airplane, the flight

attendant would tell you that in case of emergency and the oxygen masks dropped down, put yours on first.

If instead you help other people and put theirs on first, by the time that you managed to help yourself, you would probably die. To best be able to help other people we need to make sure we're taking care of our own emotions. The stronger that you take care of yourself, the stronger you will be and making sure that you can be there for other people. Again, it is not your responsibility. Everybody in your life is a strong individual who can take care of themselves, as long as they are an adult, of course. Just constantly remind yourself that though someone might be living in misery, at the end of the day, they are the one in charge of their own life.

Emotional Resilience

By now, you've mostly gathered that working through your biggest mental challenges is a task that you have to do on your own. It is not something that's entirely easy, but it is within the restrictions of your control. One method that you will be able to use to make sure that you don't have constant worry is to increase your emotional resilience. What this means is that you will be stronger in your own personal emotional management. Therefore, you won't be as affected by the triggers of things that worry you. Much of the worries that we have only exist within our mind. We have reiterated to this point that the thoughts you have are not always facts. To make sure that you are protecting yourself against certain mental roadblocks, you can increase your emotional intelligence.

Your emotional intelligence refers to your ability to understand your own thoughts and feelings, as well as the feelings of other people. There are a few different aspects to emotional intelligence that you need to understand. The first one is your self-awareness. This refers to your ability to positively reflect in a healthy way. Being self-aware does not mean being self-deprecating. You have to see the polarizing aspects of yourself, recognize the good things, and also acknowledge the bad. Don't let any one of these factors define you, and instead, discover yourself somewhere within that gray area. Another aspect of emotional intelligence is your self-regulation. This is your ability to admit that you're wrong. It is how you can look at the things that you believe and what you thought to be true and recognize whether that is reality or if that is something that is fabricated based solely on perspective. Empathy is a huge part of emotional intelligence. This is your ability to recognize and understand the feelings of other people. If you are not able to be an empathetic person, then you struggle to see other people's perspectives. You might not always agree with how people are acting, but that doesn't mean that you can't still be empathetic with why they might exhibiting some of those traits. The fourth aspect is your motivation. Are you able to self-motivate? Can you beat through procrastination on your own? The final aspect is inclusive of your social skills. Do you have the ability to interact with people in a normal unhealthy way? There are some individuals that easily lash out or emotionally respond right away when confronted with certain issues. Those with a high level of emotional resilience will be able to have all of these qualities within them that make them stronger in the face of some of life's adversities.

There are a few steps you can take to improve your emotional intelligence. One thing you can do is to make sure that you're making managing your negative emotions. This is what the book has been all about. The negative thoughts and feelings you have are what has been causing your constant worry. If you really want to overcome your anxiety, fear, and stress, then you have to begin by managing these emotions. Separate your response from your reaction. It is okay to get mad that you lost a poker game. It is not okay to punch the wall after that. It is okay to get angry with a friend. It is not okay to call her a derogatory name after that.

Your emotional resilience is going to be all about how you choose to handle the things that you feel. Of course, it's not easy. Just look at all the people who might be sitting in prison for the rest of their life all because they got angry one day and lashed out on somebody else to the point that they took their life. There are many individuals who have been experiencing intense regret over their life decisions because they reacted on emotion.

Take a breath, count to 10, walk away, and do whatever you have to do to let yourself calm down so that you can properly work through these thoughts and feelings. Identify your triggers and try to avoid them as you heal. The stronger your emotional intelligence becomes, the easier it will be to come face to face with your trigger. If you aren't quite sure what a trigger is, this is in reference to something that will set off a certain emotion. For example, if you got into a car accident as a child while driving over a bridge, either a car or a bridge could be a trigger for you. It might bring you back to that same emotion you felt when you first experienced the trauma. Pick out the things that are triggers for you. It is not just a physical object either. For example, a friend not texting you back could be a trigger because it reminds you of a previous partner who was never responding because they had been cheating on you. Getting a failing grade might be a trigger for you because it reminds you of all the negative things your parents used to tell you when you got a bad report card. Pick out these triggers and choose if you can face them and work through them, or if there's something that you simply need to avoid as you are healing.

Finally, make sure that you can practice your empathic abilities. It is very difficult sometimes to put ourselves in other people's perspective, especially when they are opposing us. People who actively disagree with you and go against everything you believe in will not always be easy to reason with, and it might just be the type of person they are. Or it might simply be because you can't recognize their perspective. Don't just walk a mile in people's shoes, walk 10 miles. Walk across the world. Walk back into their history and their past and recognize the childhood experiences that they had which could form the person that they are today. This is important to do because the more you increase your empathy for other people, the more compassion that you build for yourself.

You can't keep holding everybody on such a strict scale. When you start to form that compassion and sympathy, it's going to make your life easier. Don't say anything that to yourself that you would not say to a friend that you care about (Stahl, 2018).

Other People's Opinions

Sometimes, it's other people's opinions that can cause us the most mental anguish. You might be struggling with a certain part of your life because you simply cannot get over the thoughts and opinions of other people. It is easy to say that you don't care what other people think, but this is not always the case. Sometimes the people who emphasize this are the ones who actually care the most. It is important that we respect other people's opinions, but that doesn't mean that we have to let them define us.

Sometimes, if you are going out to a party, you might ask your friends if you look good, or if they like the dress that you're wearing. It is perfectly normal and healthy for them to give you constructive criticism so that you can honestly feel good about yourself. At the same time, if you can't handle this criticism, then it might destroy your self-esteem. Of course, it doesn't really matter if you look good in the dress based on other people's opinions. The most important thing is that you feel better. What we have to remember about this is that it is not about the words of other people that matter, but it's what you feel inside.

When somebody gives you a negative comment, or maybe makes a criticism about you, then what that does is it validates the negative perspectives that we already have about ourselves.

That's not the reality of the situation or their intention, but in our minds, it can feel true. Just because somebody says it doesn't mean that it's the entire truth about the situation, but it is common to feel this way after receiving feedback. It is how we can describe why it does hurt so bad when other people make a comment.

For example, let's say that you hate your teeth. Maybe they're crooked and yellow, and one of them is chipped. Perhaps this is a huge insecurity for you, and you have said the worst possible things you could ever imagine about yourself. You look in the mirror, day after day, and thoughts of terrible criticisms about your teeth cycle through your brain like a wheel. Then one day, no matter how small the comment is, or who said it, they simply make a tiny remark about your teeth. That one simple phrase could be enough to validate every single negative toxic thought you have had about your teeth before. When somebody else says it out loud, in your brain, you kind of register that as proof. The thoughts that we have we recognize that are not always real, but there's still always a part of us that does believe that they're true. Once we have that social proof, it pounds that idea into our brain and it is hard to reverse that. This is why you cannot let other people's opinions matter. You have to stop listening to other people. Everybody has a different perspective.

Their opinions affect their lives and their choices, and that doesn't mean that they have to affect yours. Their deepest, darkest insecurities don't have to be the same thing that you experience. We each have our own viewpoint of what life is. Everybody has a variation of the things that matter to them, and we all weigh certain things differently based on importance in our personal life.

You have to start accepting this and understanding that just because somebody else thinks that you might be a certain way does not mean it's true. Back to that example of the insecurity around your teeth, that person might also have the same exact insecurities you do, and they only made that joke as a way to self-deprecate. They don't have as big of a sensitivity to these insecurities as you might, so in their head it's not a big deal to make that joke, but in yours is the end of the world. This is why we have to understand differing perspectives.

Another thing to consider about other people's opinions is that sometimes people will bring you down just to bring themselves up. This is where strong emotional resilience will really come in handy. For example, let's say that you are a painter and you just spent all day on a beautiful painting. You reveal it to a group of friends, and everybody says that it is beautiful. There's still that one friend that has to make a comment. Maybe they make a joke about how one part looks weird or that you should have chosen a different color. Whatever they might say, it could easily hurt you if you choose to let it. What we can remind ourselves of to not feel that pain is that hurt people just want to hurt people sometimes.

It's not that your friend really thinks that your painting is bad. They are simply suffering from their own negative perspective, and they projected it onto you.

They aren't trying to bring you down and hurt you. Instead, they are only focused on bringing themselves up.

Don't let other people tear you down because they're just trying to use you as a step ladder to get to the top. Stay strong-willed, and always remind yourself that you are valuable and worthy. What matters most is based on your own perspective and how you view yourself, not at all how anybody else might see you.

Recognizing Toxic Relationships

Worry can stem from our personal relationships. There are a few things that you need to understand if you believe you are in a toxic relationship.

One issue that you might have is that you are dependent on that other person. Whether you are dependent on them to take care of you, or you have the need to take care of them, there is a chance that you are too reliant on each other. When it becomes about too much nurturing, rather than shared experiences, this is a sign that there might be some toxicity in that emotional relationship. The two of you might be so dependent on each other because you are not able to have that self-esteem or self-love. You depend on the other person because they fulfill a need within yourself that you can't find on your own. Another sign of a toxic relationship is that you shut out other people or that you've stopped doing things that you used to enjoy. This might be because you're fulfilling your identity with that other person rather than being an individual human. You are becoming fused together with that other person. It is great to have a life partner and somebody that you can always share jokes and laugh with at the same time. You don't want to become them. You should still be an individual and autonomous person within that relationship.

This is why you might have so much worry about your relationship. Perhaps you constantly fear what happens when they're not around. Maybe separation gives you anxiety and you hate not being with them as frequently as possible. This is a sign that you should change your toxic relationship.

You don't want to forget about yourself. Your husband, wife, girlfriend, boyfriend, or whoever should be a partner. It should be an equal relationship. Sometimes it might not always be equal, or split 50/50. Sometimes, perhaps, it's 20/80 or 30/70. Maybe their parents just died or they lost their job. That's when you would step in and you would take that higher responsibility for the relationship. A healthy relationship goes back and forth. You should only accept that larger responsibility because you know that things will even out again, and you also understand that if the tables were turned, they would do the same thing for you. If it's constantly a 20/80 or 90/10 relationship that is not healthy. That is a toxic thing that you need to get out of. Let's go over how you can best improve these relationships.

Improving Emotional Relationships

Sometimes, you will have to decide if you should eliminate or minimize people who have negative influence in your life.

At the end of the day, relationships should make you feel good. Of course, there are definitely going to be moments when you struggle and you'll have to fight with the other person and work through your emotions together. During your relationship, if you're not at least 80% feeling good all the time, then it's time to get out of there. It is hard to leave a relationship, and it's not easy to break things off. Don't keep yourself trapped into a relationship just because you regret spending all that time together. For example, just because you've been married to somebody for 10 years, doesn't mean you have to stay another 10 years. Just because you've already invested that time you might have this idea around relationships that there is one person forever. That's really romantic and that's great to think about, but at the same time, it creates this toxic mentality that once you do invest time with somebody, you have to stick around with them forever even if they don't fully feel like, "the one."

It's not healthy either to date a ton of people for three months, and move on over and over again. Of course, if that's what you want to do, and you're aware of that, that's perfectly fine. However, if you're doing it because you run every time a relationship gets kind of hard, that's not really good for you. A relationship will have its ups and downs, but it should be mostly ups.

It will have challenging times, but that should come from within, and you have to confront your issues and grow. A relationship shouldn't involve you constantly wishing that the other person would change.

There might be one person for us forever. But if we only think in that mentality, it means that once we do commit to somebody, we aren't allowed to break things off. So many individuals stay trapped in years of an unhealthy relationship because they're too afraid to leave. They think that they already spent their entire 20s and 30s dating them, so what's the point of leaving? If you have been happy for longer than a few years, you absolutely need to consider a drastic change. If you aren't seeking relationship therapy with them, then it's time to start with that. If you want to leave, it is okay to do so.

You shouldn't give up on people, but if you tried and exhausted all your resources, then don't only stick around because you are afraid of the time lost.

Not every relationship we have has to be one that lasts forever. It could just simply be a time that you lived and learned. It could have been a simple relationship that taught you something greater about yourself.

For example, think of a 21-year-old woman who got married to her husband, and they've been married now for 10 years. She spent her entire 20s with him, but for the past four years. She hasn't truly felt like she's in love with him. She still takes care of him. They still will kiss and hug but that intimacy is mostly gone. They had children and no longer does she feel that love connection. They've been in and out of therapy, but nothing seems to work. They've simply grown into friends. She has two options. She could stick around for the rest of her life because that's what she agreed to in her marriage vows and they have children together. That's a valid reason that many people stay together.

Then there is the other option, which is to get a divorce. She might have lost out on some time, but she got great kids out of it and learned a lot about herself. She could choose this and find someone else, maybe even having more children with that person and living a full and happy life.

It's not necessarily that she has to find somebody else either—she can simply be alone. So many individuals are afraid of that, but we really can be independent people and not have to be involved in a relationship.

Of course, every situation is different, but the point of this story is that just because 10 years have been invested in something doesn't mean that she should live in this relationship until she's 41 and still miserable 10 years later. Then what is she going to do? She'll look and say that she invested 20 years, so she sticks around until she's 51. Then she's still miserable. Well, she already put 30 years in, so may as well do another 30 more, and before you know it, she's 81 years old, and was only ever in a happy relationship for six or seven of those years. It is not as if she was entirely miserable, but the complacency can keep us in a place that doesn't fulfill the individual. When you need to leave it is okay to leave.

If you are in a place where you do want to work on the relationship, whether it's romantic or not, there are a few steps you can take to improve communication and increase that emotional connection between the two of you.

The first thing and the most important Golden Rule of all relationships is to talk it out. Communication is absolutely the strongest tool you will ever have in your relationship. Often there are simple problems between two individuals that inflate and fester and turn into a massive ugly problem because neither of the two talked about it. It could be something as simple as being annoyed that your partner doesn't put their dirty socks in the laundry hamper. This could be a small pet peeve that turns into a bigger issue the more it becomes ignored.

Eventually, all the little habits that the other partner does can be annoying, and that resentment might grow. That hatred builds within one individual's brain and the other person has no idea. How are you supposed to fix a problem if only one person is aware of the issue that's been caused by both?

Communication will be the number one way that you can solve problems. Sometimes it feels so scary to share your feelings, but what is even more terrifying is staying trapped in a loveless relationship for too long.

Another step is to look back at the beginning of the relationship and remember the good times. It sounds so cliché, but it is true. This is why keeping a journal is helpful because it reminds you of those feelings and emotions that you had and is a reminder that love does exist somewhere. You can pull it out this journal and reflect to get back into a place where you see the same perspectives you used to. If that love and compassion was genuine from the start, then you can improve on it now.

When it comes to working through problems on your own, then you have to be willing to admit that you're wrong. We can't place blame on the other partner and make it seem as though they are the one who is solely responsible for the issues within the relationship. A partnership is one where everybody accepts responsibility. Each person takes the thing that they did and acknowledges that it might have been wrong.

This is the method that you will use to increase your emotional relationship. In terms of actually talking to the other person, make sure that you use "I feel" statements. These include some things like

"I feel as though this has been happening," or "I don't feel as though I'm getting recognized enough," or "I feel underappreciated." You don't want to say "You don't recognize me enough," or "You don't appreciate me."

Once you start doing that you point the finger and you create defenses. A conversation is not a competition; both parties should come out feeling good about themselves in the end. Ensure that you do everything within your power to keep the both of you civil and happy. At the end of the day, a relationship is 50/50. If you are the one putting in all the effort and trying to increase and they're not doing anything at all, then they simply might not want to improve that relationship. Not everybody is ready to emotionally confront themselves and not everybody has the emotional meter to deal with certain issues between individuals. Take care of yourself first, and if you can help other people that's great, but remember it is not your responsibility.

Overcoming Life's Adversity in a Practical Way

Now it is time for us to get into the more practical tips for decreasing your worry. All throughout this book we have helped educate you on what is needed to be known about mental health, while also providing you with some practical methods of reworking your memories. These are going to be physical ways now that you can make sure you are relieving your stress. Whether it's a simple mindfulness activity, or a creative hobby, you can find outlets. Triggers, frustrations, and worries exist all throughout this world around you. Don't be afraid to get creative with the things that you do to decrease your stress. Of course, it's going to be a struggle sometimes, but at the end of the day, what matters most is that you are taking care of yourself and your health.

The first practical thing that you can do to decrease your worry is to be mindful. Mindfulness is the act of noticing your surroundings. Often anxiety is going to be occurring because your brain is either stuck in the past or you are fearful over what will happen in the future. When you can confront your emotions and stay true in this moment, you will work through your biggest anxieties. A simple form of mindfulness is to notice your surroundings. Start by picking out one singular color for this activity–we'll say green. Take a moment to look at everything in the room and notice all the things that are green. There you go, that's mindfulness! All it takes is recognizing the things that are around you so that your brain and your focus get pulled right back into this moment. It is not always easy and there will certainly be moments that you struggle with these emotions, but at the end of the day, you do have the power in your hands to resolve your greatest issues.

Another thing that we need to make sure we are practically doing is recognizing the food that we eat. A lot of the times, some of the food or things that you drink could be the reason that you might be experiencing anxiety. For example, too much sugar and caffeine can make your heartbeat faster, and it can increase your anxiety. Of course, having a candy bar doesn't give you anxiety, but it will inflate it. Consider the things that you're eating and how processed or additives might also be affecting your brain. Inflammation occurs within the body as a defense mechanism toward outside sources. This is why if you got a cut on your hand, it would start to get a little bit more red and inflamed. We can see that on our physical skin, but it also occurs within our body. Your brain might actually be experiencing inflammation if you only eat a diet that consists of additives. This includes things like preservatives or food colors that are not as natural to our body.

You don't have to go on an incredibly strict diet if you are anxious, but try to make better choices when you can. The food that you should include that could help alleviate some anxiety and depression are foods that are high in antioxidants.

These are things like fatty fish, spinach, or berries. Really, many fruits and vegetables will be helpful in ensuring that you don't experience too much inflammation.

Moving on from this, make sure that you discover a practical hobby that you can start. Whether it's dancing, painting, sculpting, writing, gardening, cooking, playing an instrument, or anything else, pick out something that makes you feel good about yourself. Try out as many different hobbies as you can. If you want to be a painter, try painting. If you decide you hate it, don't keep painting. It is as simple as that. Keep trying things out until you find one thing that you enjoy. Not only will it make you feel good about yourself, but it will distract you enough so that you aren't constantly ruminating or running through these anxious thoughts in your brain.

Whatever you do, always put yourself first and seek out methods that will increase your level of confidence. The better you feel about yourself, the more that will show through the things that you do.

CONCLUSION

Now that we have made it to the end of the book, it is time for you to try to answer the question yourself: is unlimited happiness really possible?

This is a complex question because it depends on the individual. There is hope by intervening on various aspects of your life to achieve happiness in small steps. As long as you are doing whatever you can within your power to make sure that you are decreasing worry, **being happy person is 100% achievable.**

It doesn't always feel like having good emotions and a happy life are possible, but we promise you that this is entirely within your range of control. As we have already mentioned, living a happy life does not mean that you were free from stress. Being the individual who doesn't have to constantly worry doesn't mean that there are still things in your life that are challenging. When we envision a happy life, we picture ourselves laying on the beach, having people feed us grapes and bring us drinks and not having a care in the world. Of course, this was a wonderful idea of life. But don't you think you would get a little sick of this after five years of laying on the same beach every day? Maybe not, but at the same time, we need to open yourself up to new experiences and altering perspectives. If you limit yourself you will find your mind falling back into the same traps. We need to seek out challenge because that means growth. Even when you fail, you can learn something from this experience.

This is what is important for us to remember throughout our entire lives. Maybe one day you'll get to that place where you can lay in bed all day and eat chocolate while you watch TV. But for now, we still have to get up in the morning, go to work, and just do basic tasks that can sometimes be draining.

Life is not about waiting for that end. You don't have to look toward retirement for that to be a happy point in your life. You can experience joy every single day that you are on this planet.

It can sound delusional, especially to a depressed and anxious mind, but if we start to rework our thoughts, one day we can get to a place where we don't have to worry so much. You can be presented with a challenge or come face to face with an issue and still be able to have a smile throughout the entire process. Being a happy and positive person doesn't mean that you ignore the bad, you simply choose to focus on the good instead.

Practice gratitude when you can, and always reflect in a healthy and productive way. It is important that we don't constantly ruminate about our regrets and our remorse.

Look back on mistakes you might have made and pull something valuable from this rather than making yourself feel ashamed.

You can live a happy life. Unlimited happiness is 100% possible. The answer is to manage your worry. Once you will reduce your worry and stress, it doesn't matter if you are somebody living in a cramped apartment with zero dollars in their bank account or a billionaire with five different private islands. Both of these individuals can be the same level of happiness.

It is not about what is around us, which makes us happy, but what exists within ourselves.

BOOK 2: EMOTIONAL QUOTIENT 2.0

Master Your Emotional Intelligence for a Better, Happier, and Healthier Life.

A Practical Guide to Raise Your EQ. (IQ+EQ=SUCCESS)

INTRODUCTION

Emotional intelligence (EI), as the name suggests, is the "capacity to legitimately reason with emotions and to utilize emotions to upgrade thought." EI alludes to a person's capacity to see, control, assess, and express emotions.

The Star Trek arrangement clarifies the Vulcans as the emotional devoid, they are known as logical beings who have expelled emotions from their everyday lives.

Vulcans are portrayed as comparative in appearance to humans being an extraterrestrial humanoid species. Contrasted and human beings, the emotional intelligence hushes up unique as a large portion of the Vulcan don't express emotion as they have them. Just the individuals who follow the order of Kolinahr have totally cleansed all emotions from their minds; most Vulcans, despite everything, have emotions, yet don't express or discharge them.

The equivalent discipline or rule applies to the

human being as being fit for dealing with and controlling the emotions depends on some key standards which fill in as a guide, systems, and strategies of being ready to expand the emotional quotient and the emotional intelligence to make progress in their regular live and in their work environment.

The arrangement includes both emotional and unemotional characters, and these prompts the following period of mind clairvoyance, which manages the mind-meld, "mind meld" is achievable by contacting another being and offer considerations, which is a not a simple assignment for human beings.

Vulcans have additionally shown clairvoyance at a huge span and through dividers. For instance, Captain Spock of the Star Trek arrangement was a half being, notwithstanding the reception of Surak's code of emotional control.

In spite of the fact that in the arrangement, not all Vulcan characters follow the way of unadulterated logic, some rather decide to grasp emotions. They are noted for their endeavor to live by logic and reason with as meager impedance from emotion.

A mind meld is a procedure for sharing contemplations, encounters, recollections, and information with another individual, basically a restricted type of clairvoyance. The Vulcans can perform mind-melds with individuals from most different species.

Emotional quotient, or your emotional intelligence, is another part of intelligence and one that can assume an urgent job in your prosperity.

Level of intelligence was accepted to be a definitive measure for accomplishment invocations and life, all in all, however, there are contemplates that show an immediate connection between higher EQ and fruitful experts. Individuals with high EQ, for the most part, accomplish more, exceed expectations at collaboration and administration, and show more drive. A few companies and enormous associations have ordered EQ tests during the contracting procedure, and have instructing workshops on emotional and social skills. Social and Emotional Learning (SEL) is increasing a ton of prominence with experts, yet additionally among understudies.

In the Vulcan way, Vulcans can embed their "Katra" into someone else by means of a mind-meld just before death. Sarek disclosed to Kirk that Spock's Katra was "his substance, everything that was not of the body, his Katra, his living soul.

PART ONE
Theory

WHAT EMOTIONS ARE

Emotions originate from the Latin expression more significantly moving. The term is a blend of vitality and movement, an expression of how life is continually in streaming movement. Emotions are something we continually feel and can happen when activities or feelings mix a specific reaction inside us. We may feel emotions from a circumstance, an encounter, or from recollections. They help us to comprehend the things we are encountering and to express the manner in which those things cause us to feel whether they are positive or negative.

Here and there, on account of injury, emotions can stall out or closed off, with the goal that when we experience them once more, we can't process or respond appropriately to them. Positive emotions are intended to strengthen an encounter as pleasant with the goal that we search it out once more. They enact the prize frameworks inside the brain, which causes us to feel safe. Negative emotions, then again, caution us of possibly perilous circumstances and raise the endurance impulses inside us with the goal that we become significantly more mindful. As it were, our emotions have advanced to assist us with making due in a more cerebral society than that of our far-off predecessors, yet the responses are particularly the equivalent.

Emotions are mental and physiological states related to a wide assortment of feelings, contemplations, and practices. Emotions are a prime determinant of the feeling of abstract prosperity and seem to assume a focal job in numerous human exercises.

For a great many people, feelings and emotions are especially the equivalents. Normally, we would see them as equivalent words, two words with a similar significance. I they are subject to one another; emotions and feelings are somewhat various things.

Emotions depict physiological states and are produced intuitively. As a rule, they are self-ruling substantial reactions to the certain outside or inner occasions. Conversely, feelings are abstract encounters of emotions and are driven by cognizant considerations and reflections. This implies we can have emotions without having feelings, be that as it may, we essentially can't have feelings without having emotions.

Primary And Secondary

Envision something has occurred, anything, and out of nowhere, you are feeling an emotion. It is solid; it is the main response to what has occurred. That is a primary emotion. Primary emotions are the body's first reaction, and they are normally extremely simple to distinguish in light of the fact that they are so solid. The most widely recognized primary emotions are dread, satisfaction, bitterness, and outrage.

These may likewise be secondary emotions given various circumstances, yet when we initially respond, it's as a rule with one of the above mentioned. On the off chance that the telephone rang and somebody began shouting at you for reasons unknown, you would most likely feel irate or apprehensive or if the telephone rang and somebody disclosed to you that your canine had passed on you would feel miserable. There doesn't need to be a colossal upgrade to inspire a primary emotion. Primary emotions are versatile in light of the fact that they cause us to respond to a specific route without being debased or inspected. They are particularly an instinctual, basic, endurance reaction.

Primary Emotions

Primary emotions are more transient than secondary emotions, which is the reason they are less confounded and more obvious. The primary thing we feel is legitimately associated with the occasion or improvement; however, over the long haul, we battle to interface a similar emotion with the occasion on the grounds that our emotions have changed.

Secondary Emotions

Secondary emotions are substantially more perplexing in light of the fact that they regularly allude to the feelings you have about the primary emotion. These are taken in emotions that we get from our parent(s) or primary guardians as we grow up. For instance, when you feel irate, you may feel embarrassed a short time later, or when you feel satisfied, you may feel alleviation or pride. In Star Wars, Master Yoda clarified secondary emotions consummately - "dread prompts outrage, outrage prompts abhor, loathe prompts languishing."

Secondary emotions can likewise be isolated into instrumental emotions. These are oblivious and constant. We learn instrumental emotions as youngsters as a type of molding. At the point when we cry, a parent comes to calm us; thus, we figure out how to utilize the outward appearances and reactions related to crying when we need that alleviating or suspicion that all is well and good.

Numerous little children are extremely capable of utilizing instrumental emotions to get their way with outrage. A baby pitches a fit, and guardians surrender to make them calm. As we get more seasoned, we discover that this conduct isn't suitable; if not, we become ruined and manipulative. By not learning the right secondary emotional reaction, it leaves the individual inaccessible and emotionally disengaged from everyone around them.

How To Tell The Difference?

Besides secondary emotions being more enthusiastically to name, there are a few different ways to determine whether you are feeling a primary emotion or a secondary one. Right off the bat, inquire as to whether the emotion is straightforwardly a response or not. In the event that it is an immediate association, at that point, it is a primary emotion. In the event that the emotion went ahead emphatically, yet that feeling has started to blur, then it is additionally likely a primary emotion; if the inverse is genuine, it's bound to be a secondary emotional response.

In the event that the emotion waits long after the occasion has occurred or even impacts new, however comparable or associated occasions, at that point, it is probably going to be secondary. On the off chance that the emotion is mind-boggling, it's quite often secondary. There is such an unbelievable marvel as tertiary emotions, yet as subtle as secondary emotions are tertiary emotions are much harder to nail down.

For kids, and even a few grown-ups, who battle to recognize their emotions, perhaps the most straightforward approaches to separate among primary and secondary emotions is to utilize cheat sheets. A cheat sheet can have a few feelings on one side (e.g., rage, jealousy, aggravation) and whether they are primary or secondary reactions on the back. The individual must conjecture, or settle on an educated choice, about whether the feelings and emotions are primary or secondary or recognize which primary emotion they have a place with.

What Use Are Primary are Secondary Emotions?

Primary and secondary emotions educate an individual a great deal regarding their emotional soundness and respectability, yet to a human services proficient, they can make analysis a lot simpler as opposed to indiscriminately tolerating an emotion, being ready to comprehend where it originates from, and the activities that hinted at that emotion can go about as a way to follow back to earlier maltreatment or awful accidents that have left emotional scars.

Finding the genuine reason behind an individual's response implies analyzing the primary emotion, while the secondary emotion will assist with seeing how the patient procedures data. Additionally, by hindering the manner of thinking and intentionally working through the inner reasons why somebody feels a specific way, they are probably going to see increasingly about themselves through a procedure that would have been altogether oblivious as of not long ago.

Another reason why recognizing emotions is significant is to have the option to respond to them appropriately. For somebody who battles with taking care of emotions or responding suitably, it is not able to express themselves can be disappointing. This, thusly, prompts outrage, and even wrath.

Which parts of the brain are "emotional"?

Sadly, there is no single brain district where the entirety of our positive or negative emotions is prepared. Notwithstanding, a few investigations recognized brain districts that are clearly associated with the preparation of both positive and negative emotions.

Emotions are created by synchronization of neural systems all through the human brain, including visual and sound-related zones in occipital and transient districts that procedure is approaching data just as self-referential zones in parietal areas. During the preparation of, for instance, cheerful improvements, these territories intently associate with the average orbitofrontal cortex.

Further, the core accumbens has been demonstrated to be dynamic when feeling want. Negative emotions, for example, stress, dread, and sicken, then again, are by and large connected with a lot further and more established brain structures, for example, the amygdala or the insula.

Are emotions extremely oblivious?

Indeed, they are.

Take the case of viewing a thriller at home – despite the fact that you are in a protected domain and there is not something to be terrified of, and you may get apprehensive and scared. Quite possibly, you may even attempt to stow away. Your body reacts with the more grounded breath, quicker heartbeat, and expanded student expansion.

Before you can begin to deliberately get mindful of dread or even react with a shout, your self-governing sensory system has just pulled the switches and set off every substantial change. This again shows emotions don't naturally bring about feelings yet that they certainly steer our activities.

Do emotions impact our reasoning?

Emotions have specific control over our considerations. "Fundamentally, our first 'read' of another circumstance is constantly focused on our emotions, feelings, and frames of mind. Thusly, our emotions are laying the foundation for the reasoning that is to come.

The way that emotions show up "pre-psychologically" (i.e., before contemplations) is quite useful. Under approaching dangers, there basically is no opportunity to think. Rather, emotions "dominate" and trigger prompt conduct reactions in split seconds, forestalling negative results. Emotions bolster basic leadership, fill in as a wellspring of inspiration to choose, and make a fitting move.

For what reason do we need emotions?

The Psychology Expert abridged the five primary reasons for emotions pleasantly: Emotions help us to make a move, to endure, strike, and maintain a strategic distance from risk, to decide, to get others. In addition, they help others to get us.

From a developmental point of view, brain structures that procedure subjective data, (for example, neocortex) are path more youthful than other brain zones that are balanced self-sufficiently, (for example, brainstem), one could state that the impact of emotions on human conduct is a lot more noteworthy contrasted with comprehension and sound choices.

Further, other human emotions influence our very own by the goodness of the data they pass on. At the point when we see somebody's outward appearance to reflect dread, we will, in general, in a split second, pay special mind to risky or perilous upgrades in the earth. In like manner, we feel great and safe when detecting bliss in others. Thus, emotions, discernment, and conduct of human beings can undoubtedly be influenced by emotional improvements.

In what capacity would emotions be able to be estimated?

What emotions are and how they are seen vary contingent upon numerous components. In this way, getting some information about their emotions may be precarious since verbal reports are apparently determined by one's awareness of inward states, social effects, and verbal capability.

One approach to dodge this is to utilize physiological measures, which are all-inclusive and more goal than verbal reports. Excitement and valence, for example, can be estimated utilizing a few subjective social strategies, for example, EEG, GSR, ECG, outward appearance investigation, or eye following.

Three components of Emotions

1. The source: an emotion originates from inside as opposed to from perception.

2. A reaction: the body reacts to the emotion with feelings.

3. The expression: how we express and emotion.

An emotion is a translation of an occasion, and the feelings are the reactions to that emotion. Our emotions control how we feel, our practices, considerations, and influence our bodies.

Steps for Anger Management

We feel an emotion (disappointment, uneasiness, outrage, and so on) that is the feeling we experience from the understanding. At that point, we make a move (conduct) in light of our convictions and feelings. Our inspiration to make a move is affected by them. We experience the emotion in our bodies (general strain, stomach hurt, cerebral pain, and so on).

We normally subdue our emotions on the grounds that by and large, we had been informed that they are awful, and we need to deny them together with our feelings. These curbed emotions and feelings remain in our bodies until we figure out how to discharge them. Covered emotions make weariness and gloom. Influence our connections and can cause genuine ailment. On the off chance that we don't discharge our past emotions, our responses to the present minute will be responses from past occasions brought to the present.

Approaches to abstain from feeling Emotions

1. Overeating. Urgent overeaters feel better when they eat, denying their emotional agony.

2. Pretending that something never occurred. Disregarding excruciating occasions with the goal that you may feel that everything is leveled out.

3. Excessive drinking of liquor. Inordinate drinking can cause you to feel to talk more, and it can cause you to feel with mental fortitude, etc.

4. Drugs can cause you to feel free, denying what you feel from excruciating encounters.

5. Tranquilizers make you are feeling increasingly endurable.

6. Exercising urgently is an interruption to abstain from feeling.

7. Always occupied so you can't feel, it is an approach to get diverted.

8. Intellectualizing and breaking down an approach to numb what an individual vibe. Thinking excessively and legitimizing is a procedure to keep away from feelings.

9. Excessive TV another way an individual can abstain from feeling.

There are more ways we dodge our feelings. We need to comprehend that the emotions are bad, not terrible, and learn approaches to recognize them, feel them, and discharge the negative emotions that are not serving us.

EMOTIONAL INTELLIGENCE

Emotional intelligence (EQ) is a higher priority than one's intelligence (IQ) in achieving achievement in their lives and professions. As people, our prosperity and the accomplishment of the calling today rely upon our capacity to peruse others' signs and respond properly to them.

In this manner, every single one of us must develop the develop emotional intelligence skills required to all the more likely comprehend, identify haggle with others — especially as the economy has gotten progressively worldwide. Something else, the achievement will evade us in our lives and professions.

"Your EQ is the degree of your capacity to comprehend others, what motivates them and how to function helpfully with them," says Howard Gardner, the powerful Harvard scholar. Five significant classes of emotional intelligence skills are perceived by specialists here.

Emotional intelligence is the thing that we use when we identify with our colleagues, have profound discussions about our associations with critical others, and endeavor to deal with a raucous or distressed youngster. It permits us to interface with others, comprehends ourselves better, and live an increasingly bona fide, sound, and upbeat life.

If there are numerous sorts of intelligence, and they are frequently associated with each other, there are some exceptionally critical contrasts between them.

The Five Categories of Emotional Intelligence (EQ)

1. Self-awareness. The capacity to perceive an emotion as it "occurs" is the way into your EQ. Developing self-awareness requires checking out your actual feelings. If you assess your emotions, you can oversee them. The significant components of self-awareness are:

♣ Emotional awareness. Your capacity to

perceive your own emotions and their belongings.

♣ Self-certainty. Sureness about your self-worth and abilities.

2. Self-guideline. You frequently have little control over when you experience emotions. You can, be that as it may, have something to do with to what extent an emotion will last by utilizing various systems to reduce negative emotions, for example, outrage, tension, or sorrow. A couple of these procedures remember reworking a circumstance for a progressively positive light, going for a long stroll and contemplation or supplication. You truly have no control over when emotions happen in your life. Nobody does. You do have a state to what extent the emotions will last, how seriously you feel them, and how you respond to an emotional circumstance. The capacity to do those things is self-guideline, and it additionally requires practice such as self-awareness.

An individual that has poor self-guideline with regards to emotional intelligence frequently invests the greater part of their energy responding to circumstances. It's practically similar to an impulse. In the case of something awful occurs, they promptly react with outrage or hate or desire or some other negative emotion. An emotionally insightful individual can perceive those emotions and choose what they need to do in every circumstance that will best serve their needs.

Self-guideline includes

- Self-control. Overseeing problematic motivations.

- Trustworthiness. Keeping up models of trustworthiness and honesty.

- Conscientiousness. Assuming liability for your very own exhibition.

- Adaptability. Dealing with change with adaptability.

- Innovation. Being available to new thoughts.

3. Inspiration. To motivate yourself for any accomplishment requires clear objectives and an inspirational demeanor. Despite the fact that you may have an inclination to either a positive or a negative disposition, you can with exertion and

practice figure out how to think all the more emphatically. In the event that you get negative musings as they happen, you can reframe them in increasingly positive terms — which will assist you with accomplishing your objectives. You may ask what inspiration and emotion share for all intents and purposes, yet inspiration is a huge piece of emotional intelligence. Inspiration is the power that pushes you to activity and drives you towards objectives. Emotion is your perspective, dependent on your circumstance and environment. Inspiration and emotion work inseparably to help move you forward throughout everyday life.

Inspiration in regards to emotional quotient identifies with your capacity to move in the direction of progress and an increasingly positive mood. We, as a whole, have negative musings or circumstances now and again, yet with inspiration, you can reframe those negative thoughts into a positive light. This region of emotional quotient additionally requires:

Inspiration is comprised of:

- Achievement drive. Your steady endeavoring to improve or to satisfy a guideline of greatness.

- Commitment. Lining up with the objectives of the gathering or association.

- Initiative. Preparing yourself to follow up on circumstances.

- Optimism. Seeking after objectives relentlessly regardless of hindrances and difficulties.

4. Empathy. The capacity to perceive how individuals feel is imperative to accomplishment in your life and vocation. The more skillful you are at perceiving the feelings behind others' signals, the better you can control the signs you send them. While the initial two components of emotional intelligence manage your very own musings and activities, empathy is the intrinsic capacity to perceive how others feel. After all, you can place yourself in the other individual's shoes and comprehend what it resembles to feel their emotions.

Empathy can possibly happen when you have a more significant level of self-awareness. You can't comprehend the emotions of someone else on the off chance that you don't sincerely have the foggiest idea what you feel. When you can feel for someone else, you are one bit nearer to a higher EQ.

A sympathetic individual exceeds expectations at:

♣ Service direction. Envisioning, perceiving, and addressing customers' needs.

♣ Developing others. Detecting what others have to advance and reinforcing their capacities.

♣ Leveraging assorted variety. Developing open doors through different individuals.

♣ Political awareness. Perusing a gathering's emotional flows and force connections.

♣ Understanding others. Recognizing

the feelings behind the necessities and needs of others.

5. Social skills. The development of good relational skills is commensurate to achievement in your life and profession. In the present constantly associated world, everybody has prompt access to technical information. In this way, "relationship building abilities" are significantly progressively significant now since you should have a high EQ to more readily comprehend, understand haggle with others in a worldwide economy. This component has to do with your connections with others. We, as a whole, know the wide feeling of social skills is the capacity to collaborate with others; however, what does that have to do with your emotional quotient?

The better you comprehend your emotions just as the emotions of everyone around you, the better you will have the option to the interface. You can utilize your awareness just as your empathy to fabricate better and more grounded associations with everyone around you, regardless of whether it's your collaborator or your relative.

Among the most valuable skills are:

♣ Influence. Employing successful influence strategies.

♣ Communication. Sending clear messages.

♣ Leadership. Rousing and controlling gatherings and individuals.

♣ Change impetus. Starting or overseeing change.

♣ Conflict management. Understanding, arranging, and settling contradictions.

♣ Building bonds. Sustaining instrumental connections.

♣ Collaboration and collaboration. Working with others toward shared objectives.

♣ Team abilities. Making bunch cooperative energy in seeking after aggregate objectives.

How Might You Improve Emotional Intelligence?

It may appear as though your emotional quotient is this enormous approaching thing you truly have no control over. Numerous individuals feel like their emotions have their very own mind, and they are in the interest of personal entertainment. While that may be valid for certain individuals, there is no reason you can work to have better emotional intelligence. It may take a great deal of work and center, yet with commitment and inspiration, you can improve after some time.

Here are only a couple of tips on the most proficient method to improve your emotional intelligence.

Work with A Professional

This isn't constantly a possibility for everybody, except it, is probably the ideal approach to improve your emotional intelligence. An advisor, therapist, or specialist can give you the instruments to all the more likely comprehend your emotions and how to function with them. They can likewise help improve your associations with others.

Make an effort Not to Judge.

Try not to rush to pass judgment on your emotions or the emotions of others, particularly when they are negative emotions. There is typically a reason behind those negative emotions, and once you investigate that, you can have a superior possibility of reframing towards a positive emotion. Emotions will travel every which way, and the better you can brave them, the more you can comprehend what to do when those feelings return.

Identify with Other Situations

Attempt to associate your emotions to different

circumstances where you have felt a similar way. In the event that you stop and look at the emotion you as of now feel and attempt to discover various occasions throughout your life that you have felt that way, you may be better prepared to deal with the circumstance. On the off chance that before you responded out of resentment, you can understand that wasn't useful and pick an alternate way in your present position.

Search for Internal Cues

Your body, for the most part, reveals to you more than you give it credit. In the event that you generally feel a pit in your stomach as you head into the workplace, that may demonstrate your activity is a wellspring of stress. Butterflies in your stomach as you converse with another person may show that you have discovered a buddy. These inward signs are associated with your emotions, and the more you can perceive that the more self-mindful you become.

Start Each Day with A Question

Ask yourself every morning, "How would I feel?" It may appear to be senseless from the start, yet it makes you delay and look at your emotions. If you do this once in the first part of the day and, at that point, check-in infrequently for the duration of the day, you can start to perceive how certain individuals or circumstances change your emotions. This gives you more data about your emotions and better devices to deal with what comes your direction.

Record it

In addition to the fact that it gets everything out of your head down on to paper, yet it additionally gives a log of sorts to past emotions and circumstances. You can, without much of a stretch, think back to how you were feeling in explicit occurrences and how you responded. Those past events can help shape your future activities and make self-guideline simpler.

The most significant thing to recollect is that your emotional quotient is definitely not a fixed state. You can impact and improve it after some time. It takes a little difficult work and devotion, yet there is no uncertainty you can improve your emotional intelligence.

THE EFFECTIVE METHOD TO MANAGE AND REDUCE YOUR NEGATIVE EMOTIONS

Opposing emotion is a common issue for certain people: precisely how are we expected to oversee pessimistic emotions that keep coming up when we're pushed or hurt? I Would it be a smart thought for us to stuff our irritation and disappointment away and envision it doesn't exist with the goal that we can restrain the result from these emotions? Would it be a smart thought for us to danger worsening the circumstance by saying or doing an unseemly thing? Unexpectedly, "stuffing emotions" is obviously not the most beneficial decision, and there are straightforward frameworks that anyone can use.

In case you've pondered how to deal with these opinions, in any case, you are not by any means the only one in doing combating with negative emotions. Various people have a comparative request concerning pressure and adjusting. At the point when they feel rout with negative emotions like hurt, frustration, or shock, they understand they shouldn't envision they don't feel anything, yet they moreover would favor not to bother negative conclusions and ruminate. Regardless, while most of us have heard that these are not valuable strategies for stress help, what various options are there?

You are right that ignoring emotions (like "stuffing your disturbance") isn't the most advantageous way to deal with oversee them. Generally speaking, that doesn't make them leave, in any case, can make them turn out in different manners. That is on the grounds that your emotions go about as critical to you that what you are doing in your life is or isn't working.

In the event that you're feeling goaded or disillusioned, this can be an indication that something needs to change. On the off chance that you don't change the conditions or thought structures that are causing these cumbersome, "cautioning" emotions, you will continue being actuated by them.

Similarly, while you are not dealing with the emotions you are feeling, they can cause issues with your physical and emotional wellbeing.

Rumination, or the tendency to pester shock, scorn, and other ungainly opinions, nevertheless, brings wellbeing results as well. So, it's basic to check out your emotions and, from that point onward, figure out how to discharge them. This is the thing that we propose.

Appreciate Your Emotions

Search inside and endeavor to pinpoint the conditions that are making the weight and negative emotions for an amazing duration.

- Negative emotions can rise out of an actuating event: an immense residual job that needs to be done, for example.

- Negative emotions are moreover the delayed consequence of our insights incorporating a period; how we interpret what happened can change how we experience the event and whether it causes pressure.

The essential control of your emotions is to get

you to see the issue with the goal that you can turn out indispensable improvements.

Change What You Can

Take what you've picked up from my first proposal and set it moving. Cut down on your weight triggers, and you'll wrap up the tendency of negative emotions less a significant part of the time.

This could include:

- Cutting down on occupation stress.

- Learning the demonstrations of certain correspondence (so you don't feel trampled by people).

- Changing negative thought structures through a methodology known as subjective revamping.

Find an Outlet

Causing changes for a mind-blowing duration can wipe out negative emotions. Be that as it may, it won't discard your weight triggers. As you make changes for a mind-blowing duration to accomplish less disappointment, you will, in like manner, need to find invigorating outlets for dealing with these emotions.

• Regular exercise can give an emotional lift similarly as an outlet for negative emotions.

• Meditation can empower you to find some internal "space" to work with, so your feelings don't feel so overwhelming.

• Finding open entryways for having some great occasions and getting all the more laughing in your life can moreover change your perspective and decrease pressure.

"Much of the time, you will find that your pressure or your feelings of fear about those conditions were exaggerated. It's so tempting to respond to uneasiness and worry with reassurance, whether or not it's in ourselves or our kids or our associates. Somebody is really worried over what's to come,"

1. Rest

Force rests have such an enormous number of preferences like boosting your invulnerable limit and decreasing muscle aggravation, notwithstanding, did you understand that can improve your manner? Dozing after dreadful events makes you less fragile to their negative emotions for the day than the people who didn't rest.

2. Talk uproariously to yourself

Self-talk is the primary concern a trooper focuses on during the situation talking uproariously to yourself using "You" not "I" when feeling awful or unmotivated. This is the thing that the assessment says:

3. Record it

Journaling your negative thoughts makes you get them. Negative emotions travel all over quickly, and journaling urges you to get them before you completely dismiss what makes you grievous or irate. Keeping a journal is astoundingly significant, especially before colossal events or on the off chance that you're someone who will when all is said in done pressure a lot.

4. Banter with a friend

"Having several partners is more hazardous than heaviness and is the indistinguishable wellbeing threat of smoking fifteen cigarettes every day. The Surprising Secret Behind Why Everything You Know About Success Is (Mostly) Wrong.

Venting out — extremely like expressive creation — causes you to feel significantly better and makes you find better solutions for your issues got together with the manner in which that you're speaking with someone who contemplates you, which you can discover in a respectable friend.

Another preferred position of having a minding care bunch is that you get a ton from grasping them. According to analyzes, grasps have such tremendous quantities of therapeutic preferences, one of which is diminishing weight.

5. Find something you're thankful for

"The fight closes when the gratefulness begins" this was what Amelia Boone, the four-time titleholder in Obstacle Racing, mentioned to be formed on an interestingly made arm adornments that she wears every day.

The best strategy to Deal with Negative Emotions at Work

It is sheltered to state that you are feeling eager, incensed, or unmitigated overwhelmed at work? Here are a couple of indications for how to manage these emotions and capitalize on your workday more.

We seem to get a kick out of grumbling about work genuinely. We float around the water cooler, trust in our partners, and even offer our workplace awfulness stories with our mates.

Regardless, relating all of the things that made us miserable one day doesn't empower us to take advantage of our workday even more tomorrow. A better procedure is to address the negative notions we have.

At whatever point bothering, self-question, or the surface of the blue at work, we can make sense of how to work through these opinions. Here are three emotion guideline frameworks you can use—and how to attempt them for progressively euphoric work life.

1. Cautious affirmation: Let be the things you can't change

Negative emotions exist. Pushing them away or dismissing them achieves more naughtiness than anything, whether or not we might be tempted to do in that capacity.

Rather, have a go at perceiving your emotions and giving them a seat at the table. Maybe you feel horrible on the grounds that your director plays top decisions—and you're not the top decision. Or then again, perhaps you're disillusioned in light of the fact that your partners are persistently running late. It's okay to feel these negative emotions. You don't need to condemn yourself.

To make sense of how to practice affirmation at work, start at home by working out an overview of the things you can and can't control. In any case, focus on the things you can't control. Allow any emotions to have risen to the surface. Work on enduring these emotions, and yourself, comparably as you appear to be—offering expressions like, "I am irate that I didn't get a progression. Nonetheless, that is okay. I am allowed to feel furious." Experience these emotions. In any case, don't grasp them or ruminate on the causes. Let them obscure time allowing.

An expression of alarm: You might be unmistakably overhauled by truly changing your situation on the off chance that you can do in that capacity, instead of enduring a damaging boss or unfortunate workplace. Use that overview of things you can control to make a move.

2. Self-isolating: Observe your condition like a "fly on the divider."

We, in general, experience unpleasant conditions, especially at work. You may ruminate about a social affair that went insufficiently, a teammate who offended you, or nonattendance of confirmation for an undertaking you exhausted your heart into. Regardless, the more you feel terrible, the more that horrendous feeling blends.

To calm these negative emotions, sanely ousting yourself from the situation is a valuable trick. To endeavor it, imagine that you're a fly on the divider, watching your time. How might you see the condition? How do the two people look— you and the other person? By developing an increasingly broad perspective, you'll routinely find that the circumstance isn't as horrendous as you presumed it was by all accounts.

An expression of alarm: Be mindful so as not to oust yourself from the condition forever normally. There are various focal points to outstanding cautiously present for your work life.

3. Reappraisal: Find the empowering focuses on negative conditions

Finding the positive in negative conditions is an especially successful emotion guideline technique when something happens at work that you judge to be heartbreaking.

To begin to change your perspective, make sense of how to defer notwithstanding something negative and consider or record on any occasion one positive. For example, did you get a basic analysis of a progressing presentation you gave or a report you made? Might you reappraise this as pleasing information for your calling development—an opportunity to make sense of how to improve next time? The more regularly you challenge yourself to find the positives, the easier it will be for your cerebrum to start seeing them isolated.

Emotional Intelligence Theories

Four branch model of EI

Mayer and Salovey's Four Branch Model of Emotional Intelligence is a useful method to imagine the diverse Emotional Intelligence Skills we took a gander at before (Mayer and Salovey, 1997; Salovey and Grewal, 2005). The two clinicians are acknowledged for concocting the term 'Emotional Intelligence' before the idea was stretched out by different scientists and later came to standard prevalence.

The Four Branch Model basically premises that

Emotional Intelligence Skills go under four classes, as demonstrated as follows. These are Perceiving Emotions, Facilitating Thought Using Emotions, Understanding Emotions, and Managing Emotions.

Seeing emotions is tied in with being mindful of and touchy to others' emotions. At the end of the day, it's about the capacity to precisely recognize emotions (yours and others) by distinguishing and unraveling emotional signs. This can be in others' faces, voices, or even in pictures (Papadogiannis et al., 2009).

Encouraging the idea of utilizing emotions happens once we distinguish and recognize emotions. Encouraging ideas utilizing emotions identifies with investigating and enrolling this 'emotional data.' At that point, joining it into our more significant level subjective capacities for upgraded basic leadership, justifying, critical thinking, and thought of others' viewpoints.

Understanding emotions are tied in with being ready to see how various emotions identify with each other, how they can change depending on the circumstances we experience, and how our feelings adjust after some time (Papadogiannis et al.,

2009). Being ready to foresee how somebody's emotions are changing through their outward appearances, their manner of speaking, etc., implies you've most likely got forceful emotional management skills. This is incredible—the capacity to comprehend emotions is especially connected to fruitful correspondence.

Overseeing emotions is the Emotional Intelligence skill that identifies with taking care of your own and others' emotions adequately. Ordinarily, emotional management and comprehension are viewed as more elevated level skills, as they depend on the initial two (Perceiving Emotions and Facilitating Thought) to work successfully. Contemplating the workplace, it's anything but difficult to perceive how dealing with your own (and others) emotions may make life simpler when confronting an upsetting cutoff time.

The Bar-On model of emotional-social intelligence (ESI)

A later commitment to Emotional Intelligence writing, Israeli clinician Reuven Bar-On's (2006)

ESI Model thinks about emotional intelligence, social skills, and their facilitators all together. The Model comprises of five interrelated abilities, skills, and conduct groups that were distinguished from scholastic writing.

In particular, they were considered in light of the fact that they were altogether seen to affect our prosperity and execution as humans (Bar-On, 2013). These 'groups' are:

1. Self-Awareness and Self-Expression;

2. Social Awareness and Interpersonal Relationships;

3. Emotional Management and Regulation;

4. Change Management; and

5. Self-Motivation.

The Bar-On model recommends that these EI abilities and skills add to how we as individuals get ourselves as well as other people, our self-expression, identify with each other, and manage regular requests (Bar-On, 2006; McCleskey, 2014). While its supporting premises remain bantered in the more extensive psychological writing, the Encyclopedia of Applied Psychology considers the Bar-On Model of ESI one of the three fundamental models of Emotional Intelligence (Spielberger, 2004).

Bar-On's work sees EI and psychological intelligence (IQ) as various, separate ideas, and he recommends that the previous is a higher priority than the last in foreseeing a person's achievement throughout everyday life. Strangely, there is neurological research on the side of this part of the ESI model. These investigations show that brain harm to regions we use for different emotional capacities and basic leadership can disable our capacity to work socially (Bechra et al., 2000; Bar-On et al., 2003).

Goleman's Model of Emotional Intelligence

Daniel Goleman is one of the most renowned names worldwide with regard to EI. His work on Emotional Intelligence skills is connected all the time to leadership and administrative capacities, and his model of EI is an augmentation of Mayer and Salovey's prior work that distinguished four

Emotional Intelligence skills. Goleman's (1995) model, as on Bar, depends on five basic factors that determine a person's EI. However, they're somewhat extraordinary:

1. Emotional self-awareness – which is fundamentally the same as Mayer and Salovey's Perceiving Emotions skill, concerns awareness of one's own feelings, and incorporates a valuation for how those feelings can influence everyone around us;

2. Self-guideline – concerns dealing with one's own emotions and anticipating their belongings, along these lines to Facilitating Thought and Managing Emotions;

3. Motivation – this spread proceeding on while experiencing impediments;

4. Empathy – which identifies with distinguishing others' emotions; and

5. Social skills – a lot of Emotional Intelligence social skills that assist us in dealing with our relational connections and inspire certain responses from them.

What Determines Emotional Intelligence?

A great deal of the EI hypotheses, similar to the ones we've quite recently taken a gander at, offer alternate points of view on what the ideas really incorporate. They have a ton in like manner, in any case, such as understanding your own emotions, those of others, and dealing with those adequately. The fundamental takeaway is that these are capacities, as opposed to static, unalterable qualities.

At a neurological level, it's conceivable to connect a portion of these EI capacities to various pieces of our brains, and we've just secured a few specialists whose reviews have indicated this. Be that as it may, this neurological connection returns a long time, to the instance of Phineas Gage—likely one of the most celebrated patients ever in present-day Psychology. Poor Phineas supported reciprocal harm to his prefrontal cortices that had an unforeseen impact. As indicated by his PCP (TalentSmart, 2018):

"He was presently eccentric, erratic, disrespectful, anxious of restriction, swaying... His physical recuperation was finished, yet the individuals who knew him as a clever, savvy, enthusiastic, industrious agent, perceived the change in mental character."

The incredible news for a large portion of us, however, is that in spite of EI having a few connections to the manner in which our brains work neurologically, a ton of it is found out through our regular encounters. Which implies it's conceivable to develop our Emotional Intelligence skills. In that sense, in this manner, it's you who chooses your Emotional Intelligence.

What are Emotional Intelligence Skills?

We should take a gander at certain instances of how EI skills look in our everyday lives, with a specific spotlight on the connection between Emotional Intelligence skills and social skills. We'll utilize both workplace models and furthermore think about what EI looks like in proficient, working connections.

Tuning in to other people

Jan works at a promoting office, and things can get somewhat furious during the brainstorming procedure. Everybody's attempting to hear their point of view heard, thinking they have the best thought. Regularly, this prompts a great deal of raised voices. At the point when Bob shows a battle thought, it's hard for him to express what is on his mind without another colleague talking over him, which exhibits next to no regard and can prompt hurt feelings.

By tranquility proposing that individuals listen discreetly to each other when they are given the floor, Jan is exhibiting forceful Emotional Intelligence. In particular, he's seeing that Bob's not taking it very well emotionally, and furthermore, he's endeavoring to oversee emotions in the room. It's both acknowledgment and viable treatment of the group's emotions affecting everything. At the point when everybody begins to hear one out another, according to Jan's proposal, it's a lot more straightforward to arrive at a useful choice together.

Encouraging idea

Daniel is a leaving examiner, and his activity, tragically, implies that occasionally individuals come back to their vehicles to discover him printing out a ticket. Throughout the years, he's found out that a legitimate "just carrying out my responsibility" frame of mind will, in general, incite negative responses from drivers. Frequently, these lead to objections to his exhibition.

At the point when drivers find Daniel printing out a ticket, he currently begins their association with a grin. He asks how they're doing, and whether they're okay, at that point, begins a talk about the climate. By distinguishing and taking care of their emotions, at that point, adjusting his correspondences system utilizing more elevated level mental procedures, he's figured out how to lessen the grievances against him by 90%. He's additionally effectively dealt with others' emotions regardless of their conceivably unreasonable conduct.

Understanding others' viewpoints

Lisa has headed toward Debby's home to restore a dress she obtained. She even brings a cut of cake since she realizes that Debby has had an exceptionally upsetting week at work. Debby's in a terrible state of mind since she's depleted, and doesn't welcome Lisa inside. Rather, she is smart and shuts the entryway on her companion when she can. Lisa is disturbed, thinking, "How frightful," as she strolls home.

During the walk, Lisa ponders the circumstance and pauses for a minute to consider how Debby's been occupied with unbelievably extended periods of time, working until 9 pm every day at the workplace. She rejects her previous considerations and perceives that Debby has quite recently been drained and somewhat exhausted. By placing herself into her companion's point of view and taking a gander at the emotional circumstance dispassionately, she's had the option to settle on a levelheaded choice about how to respond. As opposed to blowing up at Debby, she chooses to give her a well-disposed call later in the week to tell her she trusts things have gotten less boisterous.

There is an Emotional Quotient that measures non-subjective parts of an individual and the limit of an individual to endure equivocalness, vulnerability, unpredictability, and the capacity to get her/his once possess emotion just as comprehend the emotion of others Selman, et al. (2005). Otherworldly Quotient that measures the capacity of an individual to express, show and speak to profound assets, qualities and properties to improve each day execution Azizi and

Zamaniyan (2013). To put it plainly, it is more on instinctive capacities and self-awareness accordingly; it will answer "What individual is or what I am" Selman et al. (2005), and Adversity Quotient® that measures the capacities of an individual to react decidedly in any afflictions or troubles involvement with life and it additionally speaks to how well the individual arrangement and defeat the challenges and the ability to endure and overcome the difficulties experienced en route Huijuan (2009).

In association, each individual could surrender that she/he has had such sorts of intelligence. It could be valid. However, it is likewise extensive that it may be just a couple of intelligence that overwhelms an individual either, psychological intelligence, Emotional, Spiritual, or misfortune. It could be a result of the hereditary legacy that sustained by ecological impacts, customary practices, encounters, and learning. In this manner, these fill in as proof that each individual has its very own disparities and likenesses; thus, every individual is normally called as remarkable being. Notwithstanding, every individual's uniqueness may provide likewise one approach to distinguish each individual's shortcomings and qualities. For instance, an understudy is high in intelligence quotient; however, poor in the emotional quotient, there might be someone who is high in emotional quotient and otherworldly quotient yet poor in intellectual intelligence quotient and affliction quotient®.

Emotional Intelligence, Social Skills, and You

Emotional Intelligence, social skills, and relational abilities are inseparably connected. You've likely even had comparative encounters, and ideally, Lisa, Jan, and Daniel's accounts layout the association between our emotional encounters, correspondence, and practices.

As Bar-On noted, investigate from ongoing decades has uncovered that being mindful of our emotions and taking care of our feelings can be progressively basic in deciding the degree to which we prevail in numerous parts of life. Obviously, connections, emotional intelligence, and social skills unquestionably assume a tremendous job in our bliss and family connections (Gottman, 1998).

With regard to EI skills, the capacity to see and oversee emotions encourages us to adapt to strife. It does this by permitting us to envision how others are feeling and adjust our reactions so we can resolve them in a commonly advantageous manner.

Strangely, scholastics have noticed a particular positive linkage among EI and expanded relationship fulfillment (Malouff et al., 2012). What's more, this has made it workable for us to develop significant methodologies to improve our connections by developing our Emotional Intelligence skills.

EMOTIONAL INTELLIGENCE IN THE WORKPLACE

What is Emotional Intelligence in the Workplace? (Definition + Concept)

To begin with, how about we get a benchmark on what emotional intelligence is. Emotional intelligence (abbreviated to EI or EQ for emotional quotient) can be characterized as:

EQ alludes to somebody's capacity to see, comprehend and deal with their very own feelings and emotions.

Further, there are five unmistakable components of EI:

1. Self-awareness

2. Self-guideline

3. Internal (or characteristic) inspiration

4. Empathy

5. Social skills

From a look at these components, it's anything but difficult to perceive how EI applies in the workplace! Unmistakably laborers with higher self-guideline, inherent inspiration, and social skills have a major advantage over those with less. We'll turn out a portion of the reasons why this is so later in this piece.

EI was first characterized and set up as a developer in brain research, harking back to the 1990s, yet enthusiasm for it has developed exponentially from that point forward, particularly in its application in the workplace. Emotional intelligence master, Daniel Goleman shares his view on why there is such a great amount of enthusiasm on EI/EQ in the workplace:

"The enthusiasm for emotional intelligence in the workplace comes from the far-reaching acknowledgment that these capacities – self-awareness, self-management, empathy, and social skill – separate the best specialists and pioneers from the normal. This is particularly valid in jobs like the callings, and more significant level officials, where everybody is about as keen as every other person, and how individuals oversee themselves and their connections gives the best and edge.

The Importance of Developing EQ in the Workplace?

Emotional intelligence is an essential thought in the workplace for some reason. However, there are two that truly stick out:

1. It is connected to higher occupation fulfillment for those with high EI/EQ just as representatives who work with or are overseen by those with high EI/EQ.

2. It is emphatically connected with work execution.

Emotional Intelligence and The Job

Satisfaction

It's outstanding that emotional intelligence is identified with work fulfillment. Workers who are high in EI/EQ additionally will, in general, be higher in work fulfillment, the same number of studies have appeared:

- çekmecelioğlu and partners examined about 150 considered focus representatives in Istanbul and found a noteworthy positive connection between EI/EQ and interior employment fulfillment (2012).

- Similarly, high EI/EQ (explicitly high self-awareness) is adversely identified with burnout and decidedly identified with work fulfillment in individuals who work in the open part (Lee, 2017).

- Ghanian medical caretakers who were higher in emotional intelligence likewise appreciated higher occupation fulfillment (Tagoe and Quarshie, 2017).

In what capacity can Emotional Intelligence Improve Job Performance?

Notwithstanding adding to more noteworthy joy and fulfillment in representatives, higher emotional intelligence additionally adds to work execution more readily.

- Researchers found that emotional intelligence preparation helped representative profitability and brought about better assessments from management.

- Teachers with higher emotional intelligence, additionally, by and large, perform better in their employments (Mohamad and Jais, 2016).

- A 2017 examination by Pekaar and associates indicated that emotional intelligence is fundamentally related to work execution, especially the EI/EQ components of perceiving and dealing with the emotions of the self as well as other people.

You may be figuring, "How does emotional

intelligence have such an effect on work execution?" Through these seven attributes and qualities:

1. Emotional solidness (more noteworthy capacity to deal with their own emotions and endure pressure)

2. Conscientiousness (propensity to be persevering, dedicated, control driving forces)

3. Extraversion (character quality that makes individuals progressively open and better at setting up associations with others)

4. Ability EI (people's capacity to perform emotion-related practices, such as expressing emotions, sympathizing with others, and join emotion with reasoning)

5. Cognitive capacity (IQ; contemplates propose there is probably some cover between the IQ and EQ)

6. General self-adequacy (trust in the capacity to adapt to the requests of our

activity)

7. Self-appraised work execution (Bailey, 2015).

To show signs of improvement handle on understanding the significance of emotional intelligence, how about we proceed onward to certain models.

The Perfect Examples of High and Low EQ at Work

We realize that high EI/EQ in the workplace is a bit of leeway; however, how would we know it when we see it? What does it resemble?

Here are some genuine instances of high versus low EI/EQ at work from emotional intelligence mentor UshDhanak:

1. An Upset Employee Finds a Compassionate Ear

We, as a whole, get irritable some of the time, even at work, how an individual arrangement with her associates or representatives when they are having an awful day is a decent sign about her EI/EQ level.

In the event that she doesn't see the surliness, disregards the representative, intensifies the terrible mind-set, or reprimands the worker and instructs them to "wake up," she likely has low EI/EQ. On the off chance that, then again, she sees that something's happening, offers her representative sympathy and comprehension, and attempts to brighten the worker up or occupy them from their misfortunes, that is an extraordinary marker that she has high EI/EQ.

2. Individuals Listen to Each Other in Meetings

Lamentably, not all gatherings are certain and profitable; once in a while, gatherings can lapse into everybody talking simultaneously, nobody offering any information whatsoever, or-to top it all off yelling and warmed contentions.

In the event that a representative adds to any of

the above in a gathering, he is showing low emotional intelligence. On the off chance that he permits others to have their state, listens mindfully and forgoes interfering with others, and delicately yet adequately keeps everybody on task, he is most likely high in EI/EQ.

3. Individuals Express Themselves Openly

An individual who is happy with shouting out about things that are significant, and is similarly as open to tuning in to others talk about their own suppositions, is demonstrating high workplace EI/EQ. She is most likely likewise proficient at expressing her own emotions in a fitting manner and tolerating other people who express their very own emotions.

An individual who keeps things restrained or gets agitated when others can't help contradicting her at work is likely low in emotional intelligence. She may fight with her colleagues about their sentiments or-then again, anticipate that everybody should basically keep all emotions and conclusions to themselves.

4. Most Change Initiatives Work

On the off chance that a workplace is commonly high in emotional intelligence, it likely handles change well. Change activities are most likely paid attention to and did decisively.

On the other side, workplaces with low emotional intelligence are impervious to change, neglect to place in the exertion important to make change activities succeed, or even effectively harm them. Moreover, ineffectively, however, out activities show that the management group is low in EI/EQ and doesn't see how their proposed changes will influence their workers.

5. Adaptability

A workplace that offers adaptability and comprehension of the perplexing, occupied existences of association individuals is one that is most likely high in EI/EQ. Administrators and officials who acknowledge that individuals have contrasting needs and offer approaches to work more astute are showing a decent feeling of emotional intelligence.

Administrators and officials who will not

permit their workers adaptability and hold carefully to the manner in which things have consistently been done (when there is no compelling reason to do as such) are giving indications of low emotional intelligence.

6. Individuals Have the Freedom to Be Creative

So also, workplaces that permit their representatives the chance to be inventive and creative are high in EI/EQ. Allowing individuals to rehearse their imagination and consider some fresh possibilities isn't just an invite signal for representatives, it's additionally a savvy move for the workplace.

Workplaces that make their representatives stick to severe strategies and methods (once more, when there is no requirement for such severity) are low in EI/EQ. Not understanding the estimation of innovativeness and the need representatives must be creative and put resources into their work is a sign of low EI/EQ.

7. Individuals Meet Out of Work Time

At last, a great indication of emotional intelligence in the workplace is when association individuals meet outside of the workplace. Associations where workers appreciate upbeat hours, eating together, or other social exercises demonstrate that there is an elevated level of EI/EQ present.

Workplaces that don't highlight such solid bonds and those in which representatives don't get to know each other are likely low in EI/EQ. At the point when individuals are emotionally keen, they will, in general, get along and see the incentive in putting their time and vitality into workplace connections, yet individuals low in EI/EQ are commonly not keen on building quality associations with their companions (Dhanak, n.d.).

The Benefits and The Advantages of Using EQ in Business

In case you're not effectively persuaded about the advantages of utilizing EI/EQ in the workplace, here are a couple of more reasons you should focus on it!

1.   Motivation-high EI/EQ means better control of our inspiration, and maybe considerably more inspiration for our colleagues!

2.   Common vision-those high in EI/EQ can all the more adequately comprehend and speak with others, which makes it simpler to develop and keep up a typical group vision.

3.   Change-exceptionally emotionally smart individuals can deal with the pressure, vulnerability, and uneasiness that accompanies working in the business.

4.   Communication-clear correspondence is an indication of emotional intelligence, and it adds to better connections, a simpler time finding support from others, and progressively compelling influence and impact of others.

5.   Leadership-self-leadership, driving others, affecting others-these are fundamental for those in business; more on this later (Elite World Hotels, 2018).

Also, there is some worry that an excessive amount of emotional intelligence can support control and other deceptive or terrible conduct. In the event that corrupt workers have incredibly high EI/EQ, they might be enticed to utilize their emotional intelligence to control, trick, and exploit their colleagues, subordinates, and maybe even their management.

For the most part, having abundance EI/EQ isn't something anybody ought to be excessively worried about; it's considerably more typical to have excessively little than something over the top!

The Lack of EQ in the Workplace?

Talking about too little EI/EQ, you may be thinking about what an absence of emotional intelligence in the workplace resembles. There are two fundamental ways that an absence of EI/EQ can adversely affect the workplace:

1. Communication

2. Decision Making

How EQ Impacts Communication in the Workplace

An absence of EI/EQ can adversely affect correspondence in the workplace through a few components:

- Less comprehension of one's own emotions

- Less comprehension of the emotions of others

- Less viable correspondence of thoughts and emotions to other people

- Inappropriate correspondence related conduct, for example, upheavals of emotion, oversharing, or neglecting to convey significant data.

It's anything but difficult to perceive how these components sway generally speaking correspondence and, through less compelling correspondence, lower profitability, and proficiency in the workplace.

How Emotional Intelligence Affects Decision Making in the Workplace

So also, EI/EQ can significantly affect decision-production in the workplace. At the point when emotional intelligence is high, association individuals can comprehend the circumstances and logical results connection among emotions and occasions and plan successfully.

When EI/EQ is low, association individuals may encounter "coincidental emotions" encompassing decision-production. For instance, tension is a typical emotion engaged with decision-production, particularly for major decisions that will have a huge effect. Those low in EI/EQ may not comprehend the wellspring of their uneasiness or how to successfully oversee it, prompting an excess of hazard taking, insufficient hazard taking, or judgment blurred by inclination.

The Use of EQ to Manage and Address Problems in the Workplace

So, we comprehend what a need or excess of EI/EQ can do to a workplace. However, we, despite everything, need to think about how emotional intelligence can really be applied in the workplace.

There are numerous applications for EI/EQ at work, yet there are three intriguing territories where emotional intelligence mediations can be particularly successful:

- Leadership and management

- Project management

- Social work

Driving with Emotional Intelligence in Management

Emotional intelligence is maybe best and significant when applied to leadership and management; higher EI/EQ in leadership has a clever method for beginning a stream down the impact of inspiration and effectiveness in an association.

A pioneer who encapsulates and rehearses high EI/EQ can:

1. Communicate their vision all the more viably.

2. Improve their influence and rousing talking capacities.

3. Ensure fitting reactions to distressing and confounding circumstances at work.

4. Manage their very own emotions and the emotions of their representatives (to a degree).

The entirety of this leads straightforwardly (and

in a roundabout way) to a progressively proficient, successful, and beneficial workplace.

To become familiar with emotional intelligence in leadership and management, see the EI/EQ preparing assets towards the finish of this piece.

Emotional Intelligence for Project Managers

Emotional intelligence is plainly significant for pioneers and directors; however, don't belittle its significance in more companion substantial undertakings and connections. Task directors have a valid justification for focusing on their EI/EQ levels and improve them if conceivable.

To be effective, venture chiefs must have the option to...

1. Perceive emotion: capacity to perceive, take care of, and comprehend one's own emotions and others' emotions.

2. Manage emotion: the capacity to oversee successfully, control, and express emotions.

3. Decision-production: capacity to suitably apply emotion to oversee and take care of issues.

4. Achieve the best inspiration to accomplish is an inward or inherent inspiration.

5. Influence: capacity to perceive, oversee, and bring out emotions in others.

As you would have speculated, higher emotional intelligence is described by these five capacities! High EI/EQ is an absolute necessity have for venture administrators!

To get familiar with emotional intelligence in leadership and management, see the EI/EQ preparing assets towards the finish of this piece.

Utilizing Emotional Intelligence in Social Work

Emotional intelligence is particularly essential to apply in social work. Social specialists probably have the most troublesome circumstances, testing associations, and overwhelming emotional work, everything being equal.

EI/EQ, they both can be applied to improve one's skills and capacities in five center social work errands:

1. Engagement of clients/customers

2. Assessment and perception

3. Decision making

4. Collaboration and collaboration

5. Dealing with stress (Morrison, 2007)

Improvements in these five undertakings won't just permit the social specialist to work all the more adequately. However, they will likewise improve their customers' understanding and help social laborers feel increasingly positive, satisfied, and happy with their activity (Morrison, 2007).

Workplace Training in Emotional Intelligence

Obviously, EI/EQ merits investing some energy in to comprehend and improve. Fortunately, there are approaches to all the more likely to comprehend and upgrade our EI/EQ skills and capacities!

There are instructional classes and projects accessible for improving emotional intelligence in the workplace, some of which have great results.

In case you're keen on learning progressively about the sorts of preparing out there and which one may be directly for you, look at these assets:

Emotional Intelligence Matters Workshop

This workshop from the Careerstone Group is intended to support you, and your association figures out how to improve their emotional acknowledgment, emotion management, and social skills. It centers around instructing members to:

• Recognize how emotional intelligence impacts workplace connections.

• Increase self-awareness, self-management, and develop an away from relational elements.

• Use systems to oversee counterproductive inclinations.

• Communicate expertly and successfully in all circumstances.

• Identify and apply key emotional skills to an expansive assortment of workplace circumstances paying little heed to emotional pressure.

• Improve affectability to hierarchical and social prompts.

• Avoid practices that will wreck

achievement in the workplace.

- Practice powerful commitment skills for authoritative achievement.

Would we be able to Measure Emotional Intelligence in the Workplace?

Indeed! Luckily, there are numerous legitimate, dependable measures of emotional intelligence out there. Some are even equipped towards groups and workplaces.

These two instruments are probably the best measures accessible for getting a decent pointer of EI/EQ in your workplace.

The Multidimensional Assessment of Emotional Intelligence at the Workplace.

This measure takes just 20 minutes to finish and can give you a character-based proportion of the emotional intelligence of your workforce.

WHAT IS THE EMOTIONAL QUOTIENT?

Level of (Intelligence Quotient) is utilized to quantify an individual's keenness – or their capacity to reason, to take care of issues, and to think imaginatively and creatively. EQ (Emotional Quotient), then again, is a proportion of an individual's capacity to respond suitably in social circumstances. Regardless of the way that emotional intelligence is a genuinely new term, measures of emotional intelligence have demonstrated to be extremely valuable indicators of achievement in both individual and business connections.

While IQ is surely a significant pointer of progress since it portrays the capacity to adapt new skills and ideas, emotional intelligence has demonstrated to be a similarly significant device for foreseeing whether an individual will be effective inside an association. This hypothesis is being adequately applied in business and scholarly situations, and apparatuses for estimating EQ are progressively being utilized by human asset offices as a component of the selecting procedure.

Numerous partnerships have executed interior preparing and instructing projects to help representatives in fortifying their emotional skills. These projects frequently center around territories like change management and compromise, just as group building, leadership, relational skills, and official nearness. The capacity to adjust to change, for instance, has become a key component in corporate appraisals, made considerably progressively significant in the present condition of mergers and acquisitions, re-appropriating and adaptable work plans.

EQ appraisals are being utilized in different manners also.

Individuals have utilized 'Intelligence Quotient' or what is all the more famously alluded to as IQ to quantify a person's prosperity. The numbers are wildly utilized in numerous different backgrounds as a deciding element. In any case, in the later years, inquire about has additionally begun rotating around 'Emotional Intelligence Quotient' or EQ. That is on the grounds that EQ has been demonstrated to cause conduct, basic and psychological changes in an individual, consequently adding to his prosperity.

It was then expressed that sound emotional intelligence is basic to lead a fruitful and glad life. Your capacity to convey, choose, and fathom expands complex because of a higher EQ.

There are two ways of thinking when it comes to translating the connection between EQ and a person. While a few scientists express that EQ can be sustained and developed en route, not many others emphatically accept that EQ is intrinsic. Be that as it may, most arrive at an accord on the previous. There is heap trying instruments that have been explicitly intended to determine your emotional intelligence quotient. However, there are varieties in their substance and approach.

Estimating your EQ

A decent test including and grilling your situational awareness with self-acknowledgment plans to offer a progressively practical and reasonable derivation of your EQ. Any great instrument is planned to determine the four essential columns, to be specific seeing, reasoning, understanding, and overseeing or controlling emotions, on which EQ lives. A portion of the well-known strategies for testing EQ are recorded underneath, and a considerable lot of these tests can likewise be taken on the Internet.

1. The Reuven Bar-On determines and assesses satisfaction, critical thinking, stress resistance, and awareness.

2. The Multifactor Emotional Intelligence Scale is put on undertakings spinning around EQ's four columns, and their presentation is assessed.

3. The Emotional Competence Inventory takes in the appraisals, of the individuals who are the nearest to you, on your capacities. Questions are typically founded on a few emotional skills.

4. The Seligman Attributional Style Questionnaire determines cynicism and positive thinking.

Other than connections, EQ appears to have a

considerable amount of effect in the expert field also. Contemporary associations today generally send EQ testing systems on their representatives, and all the more so with the newcomers to determine their capacity to deal with management jobs. Specialists accept that people with solid emotional intelligence surely make great and powerful supervisors.

WHY THE EMOTIONAL QUOTIENT IS AS IMPORTANT AS INTELLIGENCE QUOTIENT? (IQ+EQ=SUCCESS)

Emotional Quotient (EQ) Vs. Intelligence Quotient (IQ) – Which Is More Important?

Intelligence is a term that is hard to characterize, and it can mean various things to various individuals. Intelligence is frequently characterized as the general mental capacity to learn and apply information to control your condition, just as the capacity to reason and have a conceptual idea. In instruction, Intelligence is characterized as the capacity to learn or comprehend or to manage new or testing circumstances. In brain science, it is the capacity to apply information to control one's condition or to think conceptually as estimated by target criteria; for instance, an IQ test. It is thought from inferring a mix of acquired attributes and ecological, for example, developmental and social components. General intelligence is regularly said to contain different explicit capacities like verbal capacity, capacity to apply logic in taking care of issues. There are two kinds of intelligence quotients: emotional and intelligence quotient. Emotional intelligence or emotional quotient (EQ) is characterized as the capacity or ability to see, evaluate, and deal with the emotions of one's self and of others. Intelligence quotient (IQ) is the score of an intelligence test that is a number gotten from the standardized mental preliminary of an individual's capacity to learn.

Emotional Quotient (EQ)

EQ is a proportion of one's emotional intelligence, as characterized by the capacity to utilize both emotional and subjective ideas. Emotional intelligence skills incorporate, however, are not constrained to empathy, instinct, imagination, adaptability, versatility, stress management, leadership, honesty, genuineness, intrapersonal skills, and relational skills. It includes the lower and focal areas of the brain, called the limbic framework. It additionally basically includes the amygdala, which can check everything that is transpiring minute to minute to check whether it is a risk.

The early Emotional Intelligence hypothesis was initially developed during the 1970s and 80s by the work and compositions of analysts Howard Gardner (Harvard), Peter Salovey (Yale), and John 'Jack' Mayer (New Hampshire). Emotional Intelligence is progressively applicable to hierarchical development and developing individuals, in light of the fact that the EQ standards give another approach to comprehend and survey individuals' practices, management styles, mentalities, relational skills, and potential. Emotional Intelligence is a significant thought in human assets arranging, work profiling, enrollment talking and choice, management development, client relations, and client support, and the sky is the limit from there.

Emotional Intelligence interfaces firmly with ideas of affection and otherworldliness: carrying sympathy and humanity to work, and furthermore, to 'Different Intelligence' hypothesis, which shows and measures the scope of abilities individuals have, and the way that everyone has worth.

Emotions, as a large portion of know, are an amazing asset in persuading activities. At the point when somebody accomplishes something that we don't exactly comprehend, they may instruct us to 'walk a mile from my perspective.' This is on the grounds that emotion all the time abrogates reason and makes untouchables believe that one is acting in unreasonable manners. An individual with satisfactory emotional intelligence considers the presence and intensity of emotions and sees the need in circumstances that others may discover unreasonable.

Emotional intelligence alludes to the adequacy of a person's reaction to their very own feelings or emotions and to those of others. An individual with high emotional intelligence is exceptionally proficient at comprehension and appropriately reacting in a proper manner to the subtleties of social circumstances. An emotionally smart individual can utilize their comprehension of emotion in concordance with great reasoning skills to settle on reasonable choices while keeping up great connections.

An individual with low emotional intelligence will probably confuse, deny, or dismiss the effect of human emotion that is available in practically every social circumstance. An individual with alexithymia, a serious condition of low emotional intelligence, comes up short on the verbal capacity to express emotion or to depict emotions in others. The individuals who battle with alexithymia report to clinicians feeling no emotion by any stretch of the imagination, just as an absence of dreaming, fantasizing, and inventive envisioning.

Emotional intelligence, as different parts of intelligence, lies on a wide range, with a huge edge for typical degrees of emotional intelligence. Like a test for an individual's intelligence quotient (IQ), the level or score of emotional intelligence can be determined and broke down for distinctive individuals. These tests mean to show how an individual reacts to the feelings of others, just as how he comprehends his own, how he manages social circumstances and the suitability of his reaction through a progression of inquiries that copy genuine conditions. In contrast to different types of intelligence, a few scientists accept that emotional intelligence can be instructed or prepared. They accept that with training, an individual can supplant previous low astute practices with progressively suitable ones and along these lines improve her collaborations with others just as her own personal satisfaction.

Intelligence Quotient (IQ)

Intelligence Quotient (IQ) is a number that connotes the overall intelligence of an individual; the proportion duplicated by 100 of the psychological age as provided details regarding a government-sanctioned test to the chronological age. Level of intelligence is fundamentally used to quantify one's intellectual capacities, for example, the capacity to learn or see new circumstances, how to reason through a given issue/situation, the capacity to apply information to one's present circumstances. It includes the neocortex or top bit of the brain fundamentally.

• Over 140 – Genius or nearly virtuoso

• 120 – 140 – Very predominant intelligence (Gifted)

• 110 – 119 – Superior intelligence

• 90 – 109 – Average or typical intelligence

• 80 – 89 – Dullness

• 70 – 79 – Borderline lack in intelligence

• Below 70 – Feeble-mindedness

Intelligence Quotient otherwise called IQ is a number or a check of the intelligence of an individual. In a standard IQ test, an individual's quotient of intelligence is looked at and determined based on the scores of others on a similar test. Nowadays, an ever-increasing number of individuals depend on IQ tests for a ton of reasons. The level of intelligence tests has become a parameter for instructive foundations and corporate workplaces related to character tests. Intelligence Quotients are utilized by individuals to discover an individual's psychological age, which is the people getting levels and execution abilities at a specific age. A Standard IQ test would comprise of assignments that include the utilization of mental capacity and differ on their trouble levels. The test incorporates checking of memory, reasoning force, numerical ability, definitions, and extent of reviewing information. Therapists have determined an offered age at which individuals can handle response inquiries effectively in an IQ test.

EQ Vs. Intelligence level – Which One Is More Important?

Emotional intelligence is perhaps the best indicator of progress. Truth be told, numerous examinations show that emotional intelligence is a superior pointer to progress than a higher IQ (intelligence quotient).

There are a few reasons. However, the primary reason why emotional intelligence is a superior marker is on the grounds that it shows how much an individual can oversee and change his day by day activities in regular daily existence. Level of intelligence tests doesn't test that; they simply test how quickly you can take care of an issue on paper. EQ can gauge how an individual will adapt in a genuine circumstance.

Another large contrast between emotional intelligence (EQ) and Intelligence Quotient (IQ) is that it measures how you oversee and respond with others. To lead or do a fruitful business, you should have the option to have successful and productive specialists to do your work. To do this successfully, you need to get individuals cooperating amicably, and this expects you to oversee numerous individuals' emotions. A high emotional astute individual can deal with this proficiently contrasted with a low EQ individual.

Intelligence level tests can't test this.

Likewise, individuals who can oversee others' emotions well, for the most part, have better connections socially and impractically. Individuals who have high IQs will, in general, be hostile to social or socially anomalous. Individuals with high emotional intelligence will, in general, be all the more socially acknowledged and progressively acknowledged in the public eye.

Top 5 Reasons EQ Determines Success in Life

Our emotional intelligence has such a huge effect on our achievement throughout everyday life, and it's significant that we completely develop our emotional skills. Here are the main five reasons why your emotional intelligence determines your achievement throughout everyday life.

1. EQ greatly affects accomplishment than different components.

It has been said that your IQ can get you a vocation, yet your absence of EQ can get you terminated. Your IQ represents 20% of your accomplishments throughout everyday life. Your emotional intelligence and social intelligence are a lot of more prominent determinants of the achievement you will accomplish throughout everyday life.

2. The capacity to postpone satisfaction is a primary pointer of future achievement.

Postponed satisfaction is the top indicator of future achievement. Individuals who can follow through on the cost today and postpone the prizes are significantly more prone to prevail throughout everyday life. Shockingly we have become a country looking for moment delight. This appears in our regular day to day existence in the nourishments we decide to eat, the purchase presently pay-later lifestyle, our trouble in holding fast to an activity routine, and putting mindless diversion in front of self-development.

3. High EQ prompts solid associations with others.

Our emotional skills have an immediate and significant bearing on our associations with others. We have to comprehend our feelings, where they originate from, and how to express them appropriately. We won't keep up solid connections except if we can control our emotions, convey our feelings in a helpful way, and comprehend the feelings of others.

4. Emotional wellbeing impacts physical wellbeing.

There is an immediate association between our emotional wellbeing and our physical wellbeing. In the event that our lives are loaded up with pressure, our physical wellbeing endures. It has been evaluated that well over 80% of our medical issues are pressure-related. We experience pressure essentially in light of the fact that we are not happy emotionally. We have to comprehend the connection between our emotional wellbeing and our physical wellbeing.

5. Poor EQ is connected to wrongdoing and other exploitative practices.

Lamentably, there's an immediate association between poor emotional skills and the increasing crime percentage. Youngsters who have poor emotional skills become social outsiders at a young age. They may turn into the class menace due to a hot temper. They may have figured out how to respond with clench hands as opposed to with reason. Poor social and emotional skills add to poor consideration in class, just as feelings of disappointment. Such understudies quickly fall behind in school and may, in general, befriend others in almost the same situation. The way to wrongdoing begins from the get-go throughout everyday life. While there's no uncertainty that family and condition are solid donors, the ongoing theme is poor emotional and social skills.

This is a condition where an ounce of avoidance would positively merit a pound of a fix. The expense of intercession when a youngster is in grade school is minor contrasted with the expense of imprisoning them in their adolescents and twenties.

How Do We Develop Emotional Intelligence?

We have to know our emotions. We have to develop self-awareness—the capacity to perceive feelings as they occur.

We should figure out how to deal with our emotions. Except if we figure out how to deal with our emotions, we will continually be doing combating feelings of misery and pain.

We should figure out how to motivate ourselves, learn emotional self-control, and postpone delight.

In the event that we are to prevail throughout everyday life, we have to figure out how to perceive emotions in others. We have to develop empathy; we should be sensitive to what others need or need.

Also, we have to develop our emotional intelligence, so we are fit for sound connections.

THE BENEFITS THAT AN INCREASE IN THE EMOTIONAL QUOTIENT CAN BRING TO EVERYDAY LIFE (A BETTER, HAPPIER, AND HEALTHIER LIFE).

The emotional quotient is a popular expression as of late. Over and over, it is proposed that a director ought to have a considerable lot of intelligence quotient alongside emotional intelligence so as to get successful. It is demonstrated that the viability of an association relies upon the productivity of the directors.

The emotions of a human being can be love, scorn, outrage, and satisfaction. The administrator needs to control these emotions to a limited degree so they can deal with any circumstance with tranquility. The capacity to oversee emotions is estimated through emotional quotient.

Emotional intelligence is characterized as a lot of skills or abilities, which give human asset experts, directors, and anybody in the realm of work, with a comprehensive apparatus to characterize, gauge, and develop emotional skills. Emotional intelligence can likewise be characterized as the ability to perceive our very own feelings and those of others for inspiring ourselves and overseeing emotions well in our social connections.

Emotional quotient comprises of five significant measurements:

1. Knowing one's emotions.

2. Controlling one's emotions.

3. Perceiving emotions in others (empathy).

4. Controlling emotions in others.

5. Improvement in emotional control.

KNOWING ONE'S EMOTION

Self-awareness is the capacity to perceive a

sensation or emotion the minute it happens. It isn't in every case, simple to screen one's feelings at the time, at this very moment, as it requires mindfulness. It is basic for psychological knowledge, self-comprehension, and self-acknowledgment. On the off chance that we can't see our actual feelings, it is more diligently to comprehend our emotions. Individuals who are sure about their feelings are increasingly capable of dealing with their lives and having a progressively certain feeling of their actual feelings about different choices: what employment to take, what connections to put their time in, what exercises to embrace, and what objectives to set.

CONTROLLING ONE'S EMOTION

Perceiving EMOTIONS IN OTHERS(EMPATHY)

CONTROLLING EMOTIONS IN OTHERS

IMPROVEMENT IN EMOTIONAL CONTROL

PART TWO

From theory to practice

INTRODUCTION TO STRATEGIES TO IMPROVE THE EQ

EQ alludes to Emotional Quotient, which takes a gander at the pieces of emotional intelligence that can be evaluated and estimated, and all things considered, is difficult to indicate.

EQ = Emotional quotient: Measure your emotional intelligence

Emotional intelligence (EQ) is the capacity to take advantage of your emotions and use them to improve your life. Being in contact with your feelings permits you to oversee feelings of anxiety and discuss successfully with others, two skills that improve your life both by and by and expertly. In contrast to IQ, which stays steady for a mind-blowing duration, EQ can be developed and sharpened after some time. Intelligence level and EQ have been mainstreamed since they appear to quantify something all-encompassing and valuable.

Since we like to gauge something that appears to be fun or helpful, humans have figured various _Qs that measure something extraordinary.

There is a lot of Quotients we can make to evaluate you. Now and again, they are valuable at the degree of independence, once in a while, at the degree of entire animal varieties.

Let us take a gander at these quotients individually.

On the off chance that alluring female:

It's Quotient Time, QT. 8)

Else:

It's Quotient Time.

Human intelligence is established in a hereditary code and the total transformative experience of life on earth. Neurologically, intelligence is steered or controlled by the brain and its neural augmentations in the body; one of that intelligence is psychological intelligence that is being estimated through intelligence quotient, which is regularly known as indicator of instructive accomplishments, unique needs, work execution and estimated the intellectual abilities of an individual, for example, memory, taking care of issues and numerous other subjective viewpoints, in this way it predicts, what an individual thinks or how keen an individual is, in actuality, outside the study hall or in any circumstance where an individual has a place.

Conversely, there is an Emotional Quotient that measures non-psychological parts of an individual and the limit of an individual to endure vagueness, vulnerability, unpredictability, and the capacity to get her/his once possess emotion just as comprehend the emotion of others Selman, et al. (2005). Profound Quotient that measures the capacity of an individual to express, show and speak to otherworldly assets, qualities and properties to improve each day execution

In association, each individual could yield that she/he has had such sorts of intelligence. It could be valid, yet it is likewise impressive that it may be just a couple of intelligence that rules to an individual either, subjective intelligence, Emotional, or misfortune. It could be a result of the hereditary legacy that sustained by natural impacts, conventional practices, encounters, and learning. Along these lines, these fill in as proof that each individual has its own disparities and likenesses; thus, every individual is normally called one of a kind being. Nonetheless, every individual's uniqueness may provide likewise one approach to distinguish each individual's shortcomings and qualities.

The Emotional Quotient Inventory (EQ-I) is the most generally utilized evaluation all around and is viewed as the most logically legitimate and solid proportion of emotional intelligence depends on the free survey.

The EQ-I measures 15 skills, assembled into five composite zones:

• Self-Perception

o Self-Regard

o Self-Actualization

o Emotional Self-Awareness

- Self-Expression

o Emotional Expression

o Assertiveness

o Independence

- Interpersonal

o Interpersonal Relationships

o Empathy

o Social Responsibility

- Decision Making

o Problem Solving

o Reality Testing

o Impulse Control

• Stress Management

o Stress Tolerance

o Optimism

o Flexibility

The industrially accessible instrument of the EQ-I 2. 0 has a few focal points over other emotional intelligence self-surveyed measures because of the far-reaching reports accessible. This incorporates a gathering emotional intelligence that can be utilized to survey group emotional intelligence, and there is an exhaustive 360 evaluation (EQ 360 2. 0), which can be utilized to give experiences from others' points of view into a person's emotional intelligence.

Intelligence quotient (IQ):

It started with estimating your psychological

age concerning your real age. In any case, that before long changed. Specialists chose to explore further and endeavored at taking a gander at a summed-up factor of intelligence that connects with certain subjective limits.

Scientists have proposed having various aspects to intelligence, for example, spatial cognizance, verbal familiarity, jargon, working memory, logical and numerical skills, design acknowledgment, and so forth. These angles don't straightforwardly signify 'intelligence.' I'd prefer to call attention to that intelligence is considered a reflection that relates to these elements.

At that point, there is the factor of what you have realized through understanding and your standard mental capacity. These feed into one another, and at some point, from the get-go throughout everyday life, and they start working comprehensively. So, intelligence is, to a great extent, factor on the off chance that you decide to make it variable.

Emotional Intelligence quotient (EQ):

The emotional intelligence quotient has gotten a great deal of footing as of late. It connects with your emotional development, ability to comprehend and respond to other people, and your ability to think about your own emotions.

Emotional intelligence explicitly measures your empathy, social skills, self-awareness, self-guideline, and inspiration. These are the primary perspectives that are related to solid emotional and social wellbeing.

Social intelligence quotient (SQ):

Man is a social creature – something almost every school kid has learned. It's just common that man would then discover a proportion of how socially smart one is. SQ measures how socially mindful you are, your ability to oversee complex social circumstances, social demeanors, and social convictions. I'd state it is a decent proportion of individual and social development.

Humanity quotient (HQ):

The proportion of your humanity. Whatever that implies. In any case, definitely, humanity is a major thing, so individuals worked toward estimating it. The score is registered as the proportion of proactivity and reactivity. HQ has become a famous proportion of leadership development. Inside a workspace, the workforce can be prepared on three measurements – intellectual, relational, and social. At the point when coordinated, a hotspot for viable pioneers and efficiency is made.

Consciousness quotient (SQ):

This one of a kind measure takes a gander at a considerably more practical assessment of the human limit. It measures the proportion of a brain's data handling ability to its mass. The most minimal awareness quotient would be for a solitary neuron performing one capacity inside a brain the size of the universe.

It is the proportion of data handling – bits every second.

M is the mass of the brain.

SQ is, as I would see it, exquisite and makes a plunge directly into a deliberation that may give a false representation of genuine intelligence.

Encephalization quotient (EQ):

This EQ is a serious decent estimate. It freely associates with the intelligence of an animal variety comparative with different species.

A natural measure would pose the inquiry – how huge is the brain? Yet, greater isn't in every case better. All things considered; some would oppose this idea. Size should be estimated comparative with something. We pick Brain size to body size as a proportion. Presently elephants have greater brains than humans; however, the body sizes are, to a great extent, extraordinary. The issue with this measure is that it is instinctive so natural to use it in a misguided manner. A great deal of the brain is committed to directing muscle development. More muscle and additionally moving limit would correspond with increasingly committed neurons.

Here are a few instances of unadulterated brain weight to body weight proportions:

•Human male. Brain: 1.4 kg. Weight: 75 kg. Proportion: 1.86%

•Bottle-nosed dolphin. Brain: 1.5 kg. Weight: 120 kg. Proportion: 1.25%

•Chimpanzee. Brain: 0.4 kg. Weight: 45 kg. Proportion: 0.88%

•African dark parrot. Brain: 0.0057 kg. Weight: 0.33 kg. Proportion: 1.72%

•Shrew mouse: Brain: 3 g. Weight: 30 g. Proportion: 10%

Do you perceive how the wench mouse has the best proportion? Obviously, a wench mouse isn't more intelligent than humans. Shouldn't something be said about husky individuals? Somebody who is stout will have a lower proportion, yet they are added inside the human scope of intelligence. So, body size isn't dependable all alone.

Due to these restrictions, we move to an increasingly complex measure. That is the proportion of the real brain size of an animal to its anticipated size comparative with bodyweight inside a scientific classification.

We utilize this equation for warm-blooded animals:

EQ=brain–weight (0.12 × body–weight ((2/3))

The constants in this equation are processed for warm-blooded animals. For different classes, the numbers would contrast. If you are keen on the technical parts of the recipe.

So, inside a gathering of animals, state well-evolved creatures, the proportion gives an overall proportion of how enormous the brain is to empower a subjective limit in the wake of representing the brain territories that oversee, in essence, works.

EQ is the proportion of how the brain of animal types digresses from its normal with a biologically comparative bunch. In the wake of estimating EQ, we can see these EQs:

Human – 7

Dolphin – 5.3

Chimpanzee – 2.5

Elephant – 1.87

Feline – 1.17

Pooch – 1.0

Rodent – 0.4

Bunny – 0.4

When we take a gander at savvy practices for every one of these warm-blooded animals, it bodes well to see that request.

When estimating emotional intelligence, the model report or negative testing is a proper strategy to be followed. Intelligence is characterized as the capacity and can be estimated uniquely by the appropriate responses given by individuals and by assessing the appropriate responses exactness.

1. Income nobleman's EQ-I:

This is a self-report test that is intended to assess the capabilities which consider critical thinking, stress, joy, awareness, and resilience. According to bar-on, emotional intelligence is considered a variety of non-subjective capacities, skills capabilities that impact the capacity of the individual to experience, getting by with the ecological weights and requests.

2. Seligman attributional style poll (SASQ):

This technique was really utilized as a screening test for metropolitan life, Life Insurance Company. The fundamental aim of SASQ is that measures both good faith and negativity.

3. Multifaceted emotional intelligence scale (MEIS):

MEIS is a capacity test where tests are performed by test-takers, which get to their ability to comprehend, recognize, and utilize emotions.

4. Emotional capability stock (ECI):

With a self-appraisal poll as a premise, the ECI tells individuals their individual evaluations about their capacities in various emotional skills.

Clinicians have developed various strategies to survey the different pieces of the character. At the point when the quality for estimating or surveying a specific class is solid, then that specific strategy is followed and developed.

With a similar system, different pieces of the character can likewise be estimated. In spite of the fact that clinicians utilize a specific test for estimating intelligence, there are various techniques with an alternate name, for example, execution testing, capacity testing, and measure report testing.

Regardless of the sort of test or name, such

tests would request that the individual take care of an issue and check the exactness identified with the measure. For instance, when an intelligence test is viewed as they may ask what is 70 in addition to 70, the assessed an incentive as indicated by the foundation is 140.

Aside from standard report testing, self-judgment scales can likewise be followed. At the point when self-judgment scales are followed, the people are gotten some information about their very own sentiment or self-observation without checking to its rightness in spite of checking the accuracy.

Self-judgment scales are valuable as they help to survey inward encounters, for example, states of mind and emotions. Self-judgment can be the best decision as they present the most precise feeling inside. In a similar way, to get to the capacity in emotional intelligence, there are barely any measures included, and they are an asymptomatic investigation of non-verbal exactness, the degree of emotional awareness scale, and Japanese and Caucasian brief influence acknowledgment test.

How to Assess Emotional Intelligence?

There are a few evaluation apparatuses that are used for emotional intelligence and are related to Daniel Goleman. He was the person who has worked for emotional and social skill stock or ESCI.

1. The emotional intelligence test assessed:

This is utilized to choose the kind of test for EI appraisal is utilized for most suitable use. It is acceptable to see the outcomes by Consortium for inquiring about EI in associations.

2. Technical manual ESCI:

The ESIC is utilized to chase for the latest discoveries and furthermore used to evaluate technical subtleties, for example, legitimacy and lucidness.

3. ESCI-U:

The ESCI technique is predominantly utilized in graduate school levels and universities.

4. Emotional and social ability stock (ESCI):

This technique was structured by Daniel Goleman, Hay gathering, and Richard Boyatzis. They are ones that measure emotional and social abilities and distinguishes exceptional pioneers. Preparing and accreditation for the equivalent are accessible at Hay bunch at Boston.

Emotional Intelligence Outcomes:

Emotional intelligence results are hardly any significant angles that should be learned so as to comprehend the incident. As such, here are a couple of emotional intelligence skills referenced and their relative yield.

1. Emotional self-awareness:

This is a skill that is used to comprehend or see one's emotions. The result with this skill is that the people have the capacity to recognize and one's own feelings and its effect on contemplations, power, choices, conduct, and execution at work. They additionally offer a more noteworthy self-awareness.

2. Emotional expression:

This is where one's own emotion is expressed. The result of this skill is that it brings out comprehension among different associates. The skill likewise helps in the development of trust alongside the impression of validity among colleagues.

3. Emotional awareness of others:

This is considered as a skill that is utilized to comprehend and protect other emotions. The result is that it gives a more prominent comprehension of others. It helps with helping, inspiring, reacting, drawing in, and associating with others. The other result is relational adequacy.

4. Emotional reasoning:

This is the fundamental skill which is for using emotional intelligence in basic leadership. The result of emotional reasoning is that there is improved basic leadership, where more information is accessible.

5. Emotional self-management:

This is one kind of skill where one emotion is overseen viably. The result of these skills is improved employment fulfillment and commitment. The other result is that people can adapt to high work. Relational adequacy is incredible; the presentation and efficiency are additionally upgraded.

6. Emotional management of others:

This is where emotions and temperaments are impacted by others. The result of this skill is that there is an upgraded ability to create efficiency and execution from others. There is an increased opportunity to produce fulfillment and hopefulness from others. They additionally gain the ability to manage workplace clashes that happen.

7. Emotional self-control:

This is a significant skill that is used to control compelling emotions that are experienced. The result is that they are for emotional prosperity, have the ability to have a reliable discernment even in distressing circumstances, gain the ability to bargain circumstances regardless of whatever occurs adequately.

These are barely any skills and related emotional intelligence results, which are valuable from numerous points of view. Each emotional intelligence skill and its related bit of leeway, as a result, are referenced.

These are a couple of primary perspectives. One has to think about emotional intelligence. There are various examinations, research, and techniques used for estimating and understanding emotional intelligence. The models portrayed are numerous in number, where just the capacity model with its depiction and estimation strategies are introduced previously. The emotional intelligence results, surveying, and estimating of emotional intelligence are referenced. Every one of these insights and pointers brings an away from of what EI is. There are likewise numerous different destinations that offer a total and nitty-gritty investigation about EI.

With EI, the authoritative condition can be profited in various manners. There are quantities of looks into that open up that about 90% of top leadership entertainers have upgraded EI. The higher they climb in their vocation stepping stool, the more the EI gets significant. Henceforth, emotional intelligence is obligatory among workers. To know whether the representatives are an ideal fit for the workplace condition, their EI must be evaluated.

IF there are financial scenes, EI is something that is significant for professional success, openings, to be beneficial and part more. There are numerous different sources that offer a nitty gritty depiction of the appraisal techniques alongside models. Consequently, Emotional intelligence is obligatory, and people should make a point to comprehend EI and learn not many perspectives so as to adapt up to the forthcoming pattern.

STRATEGIES TO IMPROVE EMOTIONAL QUOTIENT IN PRIVATE LIFE

Emotional intelligence, or EQ, keeps on being an inexorably mainstream skill to have in the expert world. Many might be asking why emotional intelligence keeps on expanding in significance among peers in an advancing workplace. Basically, emotional intelligence isn't a pattern. Significant organizations have arranged measurable confirmation that workers with emotional intelligence, without a doubt, influence the main concern. Indeed, organizations with workers that have significant levels of emotional intelligence see significant increments in all-out deals and profitability.

In an aggressive workplace, developing your EQ skills is indispensable to your expert achievement. The following are ten different ways to build your EQ:

1. Use a self-assured style of conveying.

Self-assured correspondence goes far toward acquiring regard without seeming to be excessively forceful or excessively uninvolved. Emotionally clever individuals realize how to impart their feelings and needs in an immediate manner while as yet regarding others.

2. React as opposed to responding to struggle.

During examples of contention, emotional upheavals and feelings of outrage are normal. The emotionally wise individual realizes how to remain quiet during unpleasant circumstances. They don't settle on incautious choices that can prompt much more serious issues. They CONCLUDED that in the midst of contention, the objective is a goal, and they settle on a cognizant decision to concentrate on guaranteeing that their activities and words are in arrangement with that.

3. Use undivided attention skills.

In discussions, emotionally smart individuals

tune in for lucidity rather than simply trusting that their turn will talk. They ensure they comprehend what is being said before reacting. They additionally focus on the nonverbal subtleties of a discussion. This forestalls misconceptions, permits the audience to react appropriately, and shows regard for the individual they are addressing.

4. Be motivated.

Emotionally smart individuals are self-motivated, and their frame of mind motivates others. They set objectives and are strong even with difficulties.

5. Practice approaches to keep up an inspirational frame of mind.

Try not to disparage the intensity of your frame of mind. A contrary disposition effectively contaminates others if an individual permit it to. Emotionally astute individuals have an awareness of the mind-sets of everyone around them and gatekeeper their mentality appropriately. They comprehend what they have to do so as to have a decent day and an idealistic standpoint. This could incorporate having an incredible breakfast or lunch, taking part in supplication or reflection during the day, or keeping positive statements at their work area or PC.

6. Practice self-awareness.

Emotionally wise individuals are self-mindful and natural. They know about their very own emotions and how they can influence people around them. They likewise get on others' emotions and non-verbal communication and utilize that data to upgrade their relational abilities.

7. Take scrutinize well.

A significant piece of expanding your emotional intelligence is to have the option to take evaluate. Rather than getting irritated or protective, high EQ individuals take a couple of seconds to comprehend where the to investigate is coming from, how it is influencing others or their own exhibition, and how they can helpfully resolve any issues.

8. Feel for other people.

Emotionally clever individuals realize how to identify. They comprehend that empathy is a characteristic that shows emotional quality, not a shortcoming. Empathy causes them to identify with others on an essentially human level. It opens the entryway for common regard and comprehension between individuals with contrasting feelings and circumstances.

9. Use leadership skills.

Emotionally astute individuals have amazing leadership skills. They have elevated expectations for themselves and set a model for others to follow. They step up and have extraordinary basic leadership and critical thinking skills. This considers a higher and progressively profitable degree of execution throughout everyday life and at work.

10. Be congenial and friendly.

Emotionally keen individuals put on a show of being agreeable. They grin and emit a positive nearness. They use proper social skills dependent on their association with whomever they are near. They have extraordinary relational skills and the ability to convey plainly, regardless of whether the correspondence is verbal or nonverbal.

A large number of these skills may appear to be most appropriate for the individuals who comprehend fundamental human brain science. While high EQ skills may come all the more effectively to normally compassionate individuals, anybody can develop them. Less sympathetic individuals simply need to work on being increasingly self-mindful and aware of how they communicate with others. By using these means, you'll be well on your way to an expansion in your emotional intelligence level.

What is the emotional guideline?

The emotional guideline is the capacity to oversee, change, and use emotions in invaluable ways. We manage emotions from numerous points of view, some sound, and some undesirable. The sound emotional guideline includes taking breaks, having discussions, letting loose a little through a leisure activity, working out, and so on. The undesirable emotional guideline includes self-hurt, starting a quarrel, drinking to maintain a strategic distance from torment, and so on.

A significant piece of the emotional guideline is the reappraisal of emotionally stacked considerations. Regardless of whether one is directing emotions in-the-minute or taking a shot at controlling repeating emotional contemplations, reappraisal addresses the "content" inside emotions. Reappraisal permits changing the understanding of recollections, overseeing consideration, and concentrating on helpful subtleties instead of ruinous subtleties, rethinking of emotions, and so on.

With emotional guideline, you can all the more likely adjust to the psychological, social, conduct, and psychological well-being needs in a specific setting in a solid development situated way. It is likewise useful in diminishing maladaptive and unseemly practices.

The emotional guideline or influence guideline, (influence alludes to the state of mind, understanding, and the "integrity versus disagreeableness" of emotion) is a piece of a more extensive structure called self-guideline.

Self-guideline incorporates everything from your battle or flight reaction to reflection, including how your thoughtful sensory system reacts to undermining upgrades and how your parasympathetic sensory system attempts to reestablish ideal working. It incorporates everyday schedules that help adapt to pressure. It incorporates how you act in social circumstances. It incorporates how you manage clashes. You get the point, right? One approach to conceptualize self-guideline is "All psychological and physical exercises, cognizant or oblivious, which help screen, change, and control considerations, conduct, and emotions."

That is a significant wide perspective on, so we are going to concentrate on emotional self-guideline or emotional guidelines. Aside from what we do in our everyday lives depend on our experience of what works for us, there are some extra strategies you can use to manage pressure, oversee nervousness, adapt to bitterness and torment, and recapture lucidity in thought.

How about we get right to it now, here are seven amazing proof-based emotional guideline strategies.

Seven profoundly focused on emotional guideline and self-guideline skills

There are truly 100s of ways you can manage emotions. A few methods are basic exercises like viewing Netflix, and some are unpredictable long-haul exercises like making another life full of significance and reason. On the off chance that improving your general prosperity, joy, and life-fulfillment is your objective.

We can't experience every one of them, so we see procedures to manage emotions that you can use on request.

A portion of these methods need a smidgen of training, and that is the reason I need you to regard this post as a lot of directions rather than some shallow psychological counsel.

I you truly need to deal with your own emotions valuable and figure out how to adapt to upsetting tension inciting musings, you have to figure out how to execute these emotional and self-guideline systems. Just expending this data won't help.

This implies you are very brave to do.

1. Utilize third individual self-talk and allude to yourself by your very own name
Research shows that self-talk, when done in the

third individual, can be a viable strategy for emotional self-guideline. It gives the fundamental psychological separation between the self and uneasiness initiating settings. This likewise helps when you are considering negative occasions, and ruminating uneasiness was ridden musings. This psychological separation permits an individual to think about themselves in a less emotional manner, like how they would consider some other individual. The self is regularly emotionally charged in snapshots of uneasiness.

The procedure is straight-forward. Rather than 'I, me, and we' you can utilize 'Your name, he, she, them). Here is a model – I am sickening that can change to Aditya is disturbing.

I prescribe that you read this post, which depicts why this works. In the event which you would prefer not to understand it, here is a short recap – Talking in the third individual builds the translation level. The interpretation level depicts the profundity at which you process thoughts, ideas, subtleties, and so forth.

The high translation is inaccessible, unique, and worldwide. For instance – I am getting a charge out of sports at this moment. The subtleties are ambiguous; however, the embodiment is caught.

Expanding the translation by utilizing your very own name, or expounding on yourself in the third individual, or tending to yourself as he/she/they can build the understanding level.

A significant level of understanding makes it simpler to apply control self-control and emotional control. It likewise creates more negative assessments of exercises which undermine self-control. This may assist you with discontinued or withdraw from exercises which upset self-control.

Best utilized for: Managing outrage, stress, nervousness, and the power everything being equal

2. Convert emotionally stacked musings into practical concerns

This is a two-pronged methodology that can undoubtedly help with mild social tension and apprehension. It is likewise a long-term propensity that can cradle against serious nervousness.

1.   Mindfulness and naming: In this progression, you start rewording your unique

situation and abridge your musings in any capacity you can.

2.   Constructive rethinking: You take your considerations and synopsis and afterward reword it in the most valuable manner conceivable. Rather than going 'poop is hitting the fan, and I have messed up' you can utilize 'Things are not looking acceptable, and I have to accomplish something. What would I be able to do? Will it help on the off chance that I do XYZ? There is no reason for thinking about the finish of everything. How might I fix the circumstance?'

Best utilized for: Dealing with pressure, disappointment, social nervousness, and relational clash.

3. Utilize organized breathing to control your body and lessen apparent agony

Follow the following four stages to realize how to inhale profoundly to manage tension and related emotions.

1.   Breathe in profound from your nose gradually and tenderly

2.	Breathe out profound from your mouth gradually and tenderly

3.	Count 1 to 5 while taking in and out on the off chance that it makes a difference

4.	Close your eyes and concentrate on your relaxing

Profound breathing works with various pathways. It offers good psychological ways from the uneasiness instigating setting. It neutralizes the physiological reactions of nervousness – expanded pulse, sweat-soaked palms, freeze reaction, solid pressure, and so on. Self-guided moderate and profound breathing likewise decreases torment.

So, profound breathing is useful in lightening torment and unwinding. It tends to be a handly self-administrative instrument for any individual whose appearances are devastating nervousness, social tension, alarm assaults, outrageous mental inconvenience, or physical agony incited psychological distress.

Best utilized for: Relaxing and overseeing torment.

4. Sharpen your Interoceptive sense to comprehend your body's responses

We have numerous faculties, and one of the lesser-realized ones is Interoception. It is that sense which depicts materially sensations and the subtleties of interior working as for the communication between the brain and the body.

Being mindful of these substantial sensations (excitement, breathing, muscle strain, pulse, perspiring, and so forth.), or having interoceptive awareness, is significant in emotional guidelines since this awareness downregulates influence and helps the neural preparing behind self-guideline. This implies being mindful of your substantial sensations can encourage by and large emotional guidelines.

Interoceptive awareness can assist you in handling the signs which trigger or enhance emotions in advance, and it can assist you in altering your consideration regarding valuable exercises.

Luckily, there is a strategy to improve one's interoceptive awareness. It is called Mindful

Awareness Body-situated Therapy (or MABT). Here is the manner by which you can take a shot at the 3 phases:

1. Awareness: Learn about real sensation, where they occur, why they occur. Figure out how to express them in words and portray a sensation.

2. Access: Use procedures to guide your consideration regarding center around real sensations. You can start by getting mindful of your own breathing and the related body development. You would then be able to concentrate on the adjustment in your muscle strain. You can guide your hand to contact and detect your inward experience all things considered. For instance, finishing the worried muscle with your fingers can produce an awareness of what's going on. Muscle unwinding is a key part of managing emotions which have a pressure and nervousness component. When that is done, the most significant advance is to

continue your awareness since that is when a great many people gain some new useful knowledge about themselves or their experience.

3. Reappraisal: Reevaluate your experience and circumstance to alter your reaction to the experience. This progression includes a wide range of psychological reappraisal, including semantic transformation, third-individual self-talk, and directing your thoughtfulness regarding center around fitting subtleties.

With regards to managing complex emotions, there is a distinction between your emotions and your awareness of everything else, including your body. MABT can help diminish this separation and convert it into a body-emotion commitment.

A related emotional guideline skill is mindfulness. Mindfulness preparation is helpful in debilitating a dread reaction. In the investigation, members encountered a lessened dread reaction dependent on mindfulness-yoga contemplation, which included attentional guidelines and tactile awareness. Yoga, as a general movement, is verifiably valuable in improving personal satisfaction and emotional prosperity.

5. Tune in to music

The decision of music is significant. Be that as it may, not in the customary Genre sense. Tuning in to music you are a devotee of has more advantages. For instance, IF you are a devotee of overwhelming metal music, substantial metal can assist you with preparing outrage valuably.

In the event that you are feeling tragic and you tune in to pitiful music, the coinciding between your emotion and state of mind can help with the guideline. Pitiful music doesn't really actuate bitterness. Truth be told, it can cause us to feel better Research focuses on three normal impacts of tuning in to tragic music – sweet distress (positive feelings related to trouble), elevating and ameliorating distress (improves the state of mind), and certified misery (an encounter of bitterness).

Music and emotions have a bi-directional relationship. The decision of music can influence your state of mind, and your mindset can influence your decision. The vast majority have a natural feeling of what they need from music. In this way, this is a significant simple approach to control emotions.

With regards to your association with music with regards to the emotional guideline, there are two significant elements to consider – subjective reappraisal and expressive concealment. Intellectual reappraisal resembles the semantic transformation procedure where you change the manner in which you decipher and process emotional contemplations. Expressive concealment is changing the conduct reaction (snapping, pulling back, fits of rage, and so forth.) by deliberately halting an undesired reaction. Research shows that music improves prosperity in the event that it is utilized as an emotional guideline methodology. Yet, just when utilizing psychological reappraisal. It can effectively affect prosperity if your go-to system is expressive concealment.

Music can go about as an interruption and help separation yourself from the emotionally stacked setting. It can cause you to introspect, which is an essential condition for psychological reappraisal. It likewise advances unwinding and joy. In addition, music might be a perfect ally for other emotional guideline skills. These elements, as indicated by look into, impact self-guideline, emotional guideline, subjective guideline, and wellbeing.

Shouldn't something be said about emotional guidelines in damaged kids? It might be difficult to prepare them in breathing and third-individual self-talk, so what might you do? The appropriate response might be music, once more. Music can be a viable latently actuated dynamic type of emotional guideline for youngsters.

6. Associate with nature and regular lifeforms

I'll keep this one short. Humans have a characteristic partiality to associate with nature, and it's living things. This incorporates wild creatures, pets, plants, fowls, biological systems, rocks, grass, mountains, mists, regular light, and so forth. Research shows that associating with nature can improve one's mind-set, help manage pressure and nervousness, adapt to discouragement, and improve personal satisfaction.

It's not simply nature, even fake conditions like workplaces and houses with characteristic components can help. Shouldn't something be said about virtual conditions like games, recordings, photographs, and augmented realities? Turns out, they, as well, positively affect psychological well-being and emotions by and large, yet with lesser strength.

This wonder of having a characteristic inclination to associate with nature is called Biophilia, and following up on one's biophilia can be useful for emotional wellness and in general prosperity. Watch and retain regular components by mean of every one of your faculties as much as you can.

Best utilized for: Improving by and large prosperity, overseeing the state of mind, and adapting to emotional wellness issues.

7. Figure out how to endure aversive emotions

We frequently need to endure unsavory emotions. We've just observed that profound breathing can help deal with the accomplished agony. Shouldn't something be said about other undesirable or aversive emotions like blame, tension, foreseen disaster, foreseen disappointment, and expected results which reverberate with low self-regard? These emotions structure a significant center of tarrying and lingering like practices.

Berking and Whitley portray a quite helpful strategy for managing these aversive emotions. Adhere to these guidelines to figure out how to endure negative emotions, and subsequently, emphatically influence conduct.

1.   First, you bring negative emotions into awareness, don't stifle them

2.   Instruct yourself to endure the emotions

3.   Address the setting of these emotions – does it include low self-regard, does it include others, does it include a dread of disappointment, and so on?

4.   Tell yourself you are flexible and solid

Terrible emotional guideline procedures which likely won't help

There are various things we do to control emotions, which are viewed as unfortunate. Toward one side of the range, we have things like utilizing humor, and on the other, we have things like diversion transforming into constant unpleasantness.

So, what are some unfortunate emotional and self-guideline ways of dealing with stress?

1.   Redirecting disdain and dissatisfaction onto another person

2.   Excessive smoking, drinking, or self-subverting practices that occupy you from the emotional pain at the end of the day make another arrangement of issues.

3.   Wild expressions of outrage to come to a meaningful conclusion

4.   Catharsis. Yes, there is some reason to accept that generally realized cleansing exercises like yelling into a cushion and punching something lifeless can compound the situation. In a perfect world, purge, or all the more explicitly 'abreaction,'

ought to be finished with a specialist who would advise be able to better.

Approaches To Train and R Your Empathy

Affect and Emotion, Mental instruments, Tips, and Tricks

Empathy is an attractive human attribute, and it is vital to connections, network prosperity, and expert development. In what individuals call emotional intelligence – the affectability and the skill to manage, comprehend, and use emotions – empathy is a vital power.

In some way or another, empathy is characteristic. A great many people know that others have novel feelings and contemplations. The vast majority can resound with some others on those feelings and musings. It's hard-wired. Individuals likewise realize that humans have comparative emotions and where it counts, they are not excessively unique from one another –

comparative instabilities, comparative objectives, and comparable responses drive a great deal of human holding. The entirety of this is a piece of what analysts call "the hypothesis of mind."

Be that as it may, on another level, we could all effectively utilize more empathy. Not simply in the feeling sense, in a progressively intellectual full of the feeling way – to guide choices, to engage others, to develop connections, to determine clashes, to promote, and so on

The Empathy and The Theory of Mind.

Empathy has four components.

- A psychological and thinking ability to comprehend and receive alternate points of view

- An ability to self-control conduct and emotions while monitoring the birthplace of musings, emotions, and practices (self as well as other people)

- A full of feeling (emotional) ability to react and reasonably respond to other's emotions

- A social ability to share emotions suitably.

These components are grounded in a bigger system called The Theory of mind – the capacity to property mentalities, considerations, convictions, points of view, and encounters to yourself, and the ability to comprehend that others can have various frames of mind, musings, convictions, viewpoints, and encounters. Empathy is very significant with regards to understanding the idea of torment and saw torment.

Empathic discussions have various regular qualities: tolerating other's contemplations, recognizing and approving others, endeavors to comprehend another perspective, assembling the certainty that an individual is tuning in and not simply hearing, and so on. Average explanations start with "I can envision what that resembles," "I comprehend what you are stating/feeling," and so forth. Any slang variations of these sentences fill in also.

What's more, here is the kicker – empathy, just as expressed empathy is plastic – that implies it tends to be prepared and developed with intentional exertion. Your brain will physically adjust itself a smidgen to suit empathic skills, regardless of whether you have brain-harm.

In lieu of that, let us take a gander at certain exercises to assist individuals with improving and encourage empathy. For some individuals, it's not the absence of empathy, and it's the absence of expanding and utilizing empathy. These systems will assist you with expanding your ability to sympathize well with the capacity to express empathy.

Empathy preparing systems for grown-ups, teenagers, and elderly folks individuals

1. Peruse scholarly fiction: Reading anecdotal stories impacts the hypothesis of mind, empathy, demeanor, and character. It's very healthy as a

pastime, and a propensity for perusing can allegorically place you from another person's point of view. Regardless of whether you don't recall the subtleties of a story, it affects you since you get the chance to encounter accounts in a close manner.

2. Figure out how to perceive outward appearances: A huge piece of empathy perceives outward appearances, verbal signals like emotional words, and emotional settings. Learning to distinguish emotional components in discussions can improve your empathic reaction. Gain proficiency with the importance of emoticons, watch on-screen characters, watch faces, notice changes in the eyes, watch expressions nearby communicated in language. Focus on everything that makes us human.

3. Take acting exercises: Acting includes taking up a lot of attributes and character characteristics that don't really have a place with you. Entertainers train for a considerable length of time and figure out how to put on a persuading face. Now and then they draw from their very own understanding to reverberate (talked about later) and now and again they direct outward appearances, non-verbal communication, voice, and so on to coordinate a setting in a close to true

way – Keanu took exercises from the US Marines to prepare for John Wick. Learning the proper behavior shows individuals a great deal about inconspicuous socio-intellectual highlights that are inserted in the public arena – words, expressions, give and takes, getting on signals, and so forth. These components meet up to lift empathy and the hypothesis of mind.

4. The Friend's sight procedure: Think of any individual you are near. There is a solid possibility that you discover significantly more about this individual than simply true information. You presumably know this present individual's demeanor toward social causes, mannerisms, and a few encounters which shape them. Utilize this information as a figurative focal point and pose the inquiry, "What might XYZ do/feel?" This inquiry will constrain you to consider a channel thoroughly. This channel is the portrayal of that individual in your brain. It'll assist you with turning into a conceptual rendition of that individual, and you'll increase another point of view. Utilizing this method will likewise assist you with encountering a minute with a changed arrangement of propensities, qualities, and meticulousness – individuals center around various subtleties of an encounter. That is one reason we as a whole decipher occasions

contrastingly and respond in special manners.

5. Uncertainty your translation: We naturally experience the world in specific manners, and those are (without sounding agnostic) our ways. To improve your empathic skills, you can compel an adjustment in your translation by posing the inquiry, "In what other way would I be able to decipher this?" Begin by deciphering the littlest subtleties in an unexpected way. The objective here is to change your discernment bit by bit until you have a totally alternate point of view. Once in awhile, this is simple. You can accept an alternate translation without changing any detail. Here and there, you have to differ the emotional heap of understanding to increase some new viewpoint. Something emotionally overwhelming for you can be nonpartisan for another person, and something paltry for you can be a serious deal to someone else.

6. Control words: Spot suppositions, questions, illustrations, tales, actualities, and so on in a sentence or another person's contention. Everything separated from realities is variable and can be deciphered in more than one way. That is the point at which you can see another person's perspective. Work on doing this with a companion

and attempt to populate an assortment of understandings by evolving words. Here is a model: "I was talking a few days ago, and my companion was getting all bothered up for reasons unknown."

This sentence can be separated into a couple of actualities and a couple of questions. You can change the words in the guide to feature what the realities are and aren't.

Realities: There were, at any rate, two individuals. One was talking. One seemed bothered up to the next. The two individuals are companions. "No reason" is a suspicion. "Talking" is variable.

One had all the earmarks of being exasperated up, yet no association can be drawn. The reason is obscure. The connection between talking and irritating up isn't plainly settled, nor is there more data in the announcement.

They are isolating the knowns from the questions all you to investigate new conceivable outcomes. Maybe the companion was exasperated up on account of another person, maybe the bothered-up companion can't clarify, maybe the talking companion was anticipating, or perhaps distorting the discussion (while talking, your consideration can be completely involved, and you could be incognizant in regards to your own conduct). For our situation, the word talking could be shouting without awareness, and that adjustment in stating clarifies the circumstance.

This will assist you with populating new viewpoints, and those will influence your capacity to think from various perspectives.

7. Know the hypothesis of mind: Knowing that everything everybody says accompanies a foundation story and foundation data can be sufficient for you to expand your empathy. There are propensities, frames of mind, encounters, suppositions, information, and so on behind everybody's musings. A few people probably won't need empathic capacities, so preparing isn't the arrangement. Those capacities could be hindered or obstructed by other contending musings – like coming to a meaningful conclusion and putting yourself at the focal point of the discussion. A periodic reminder to follow up on the hypothesis of mind is sufficient to increment expressed empathy.

8. Reword and Acknowledge/Active-Empathic Listening: In a discussion, the speaker doesn't generally have the foggiest idea about what the audience is understanding. One approach to take care of this issue is to rethink the quintessence of what the speaker said. Doing this can assist you with improving as an audience, recognize the speaker, and improve the subjective component of empathy – the capacity to utilize words and incorporate them into an empathic idea.

9. Distinguish Intentions: Very regularly, the veracity of what others are stating isn't the objective of correspondence. The objective is to be heard. So, learn from others for what it is – something to be heard – in light of goal, not accurate precision. Notice physical developments since they relate to goals.

10. Abstain from polarizing: Bombarding with a contrary view, frequently causes another person to feel rejected, which undermines their self-idea and experiential information, which has formed them. This shows up as individual risk, and the mind goes into safeguarding their unique POV, which further reinforces. So not doing this assist with acclimatizing more perspectives. Humans love

divisions, and one view regularly inspires a reactionary view that is pointlessly outrageous and enraptured. You'll see this a great deal in political discussions. People experience a cycle of the proposal, the absolute opposite, and the combination – Someone says something (proposition), others differ and state the inverse (direct opposite), and afterward, they accommodate on the grounds that the two positions have benefits and bad marks (union). You can frame your direct opposite; however, effectively search out a union.

11. Work on pivoting objects: The capacity to physically observe and envision shapes and areas from an alternate point helps in actuating empathy. This happens on the grounds that the capacity to have an exacting perspective is related to the capacity to have a figurative perspective. The two offer some regular neural instruments.

How to improve your memory and recalling limit?

Learning, Memory, Self-development

Here are a few hints and deceives to improve your memory – general capacity to recall, and the skill of remembering explicit things. At the point when we talk about improving memory, two things ring a bell. These are two special parts of memory.

Let me separate these two parts of memory first:

Concentrates in Psychology show these as various elements of memory.

•Committing to memory – this is the capacity to recollect subtleties in valuable manners. We usually allude to this as memory.

•Learning data – when our brain gets data from our faculties, the brain gets some pre-memory crude data.

Contingent upon the helpfulness of the data and consideration paid to that data, a memory begins shaping. That essentially implies that this data leaves an engraving at the biological level in the brain. This engraving is a little change in how neurons impart. Presently envision that there is a huge system of neurons. They all speak with one another through neural connections. The more vigorous this system is, and its neural connections are, the better the data is 'kept up.'

Procedures to improve your memory!

Recollections are put away everywhere throughout the brain, and new neurons are delivered alongside new associations routinely to help suit new recollections. So, we don't generally have a capacity unit in the brain, the memory is simply there, everywhere!

Memory has the accompanying components:

1.Neural examples that fire in one of a kind ways

2.The quality of correspondence between neurons (I won't get into the neuroscience of that here)

3.Ability to rehash a similar example of terminating to bring out a similar memory

4.A learning perspective which is using that memory for directing conduct, performing, procuring new data, and so forth.

What can you do about improving memory?

Advance the quality of neural terminating:

These are mental exercises you can chip away at to improve your memory by and large. Influence these ground-breaking systems in the event that you need to improve your memory by and large.

Anything that lets one use memory-related neural hardware again and would give the brain a sign that the circuit is valuable. So, at that point, it will set the memory on a way of fortifying itself. There are numerous ways we can use this. The more you reinforce it, the better the memory is.

1. Rehashing data:

Basically, rehashing data CAN (yet not really) improves the memory for it. Like a rundown of drugs. Subtleties of a discussion or a talk. You can rehash it in your mind, rehash it to a companion, or even instruct it to somebody. There is a method called separated redundancy where you rehash data after a brief span to reinforce it. You at that point rehash it after a marginally longer length, and you continue expanding the span – For instance, rehash names of star bunches directly after you learn them, at that point in a short time, at that point in 15, at that point in 60 minutes, at that point in 4 hours, at that point in 10 hours, at that point the following day, at that point the following week. When it's seven days gone, you'll have it retained. You can generally think back and affirm the data when you rehash it.

2. Conscious symbolism:

Popular and successful. Did you realize that the mind's eye is fit for conjuring plenty of subtleties? Envisioning something makes a solid engraving in the brain. More the subtleties, the better it is. Loads of data can have mental symbolism. Learning a graph or a procedure in a talk? Envision it a couple of times, venture through it in your mind. This should be possible in a hurry. Each time, you improve its memory.

3. Affiliations:

The brain truly prefers to make a system of things. Making the relationship between related bits of data in a hurry can hugely improve memory arrangement. More grounded the affiliations, better the memory for all things related. You can make a relationship between discussions, places you've visited, individuals you've met, hypotheses you've learned. You can make relationships by looking into, discovering likenesses, connecting them in imaginative ways, and so on. This structure the premise of the snowballing procedure I utilize a great deal.

4. Practice:

Performers, performers, memory champions, chess aces, sprinters, footballers, speakers, essayists, professionals, and so forth practice their exchange. They rehash it a million times, and they attempt distinctive yet related things, they gain understanding. All with the impact of having incredible memory and learning of their exchange. Anything can be your exchange. There are approaches to rehearse well – practice an assortment of related things, gain from models, imaginatively approach your exchange, get criticism, and so forth. Particularly ground-breaking for things, including your body. It is likewise extremely helpful in developing particular hardware in the brain to obtain 'new data' significant to your exchange (and now and then related stuff). This new data is probably going to frame an extremely solid memory. A practiced artist can remember new tunes effectively. An accomplished electrical specialist can remember complex circuits effectively. It's everything practice. Additionally, join a practice with piecing (talked about later), and you'll be a great idea to go!

5. Appoint extra importance:

There are a number of things that can add importance to data, and one can compose a book on it. Here is a beginning. Placing data in a story setting, utilizing new jargon in discussions, looking at something with companions, playing make-conviction with data, and so on. This is the place you can be imaginative. Here is a reality – there are 1,77,147 different ways to tie a tie hitch. You can discuss this with your companions. You can peruse up progressively about it. You can look into math. You can contrast it with what number of practical ways there are, and so on. The entirety of this, not simply strengthens the memory, it gives the reality a unique circumstance. This setting includes meaning. Need to recall the garments of your companions? Allocate importance to it, dependent on how it draws out their character, how it affects you.

6. Snowballing:

My undisputed top choice. At the point when you get a touch of data, fortify it by shaping affiliations. In any case, don't stop there. Keep making an ever-increasing number of affiliations, assemble more data, adapt new things, retain new viewpoints, extend your insight into it. At last, you'll structure an enormous system. The denser the system, the more grounded the memory for everything in that system. Making a system additionally helps manufacture neural hardware across a wide range of areas of the brain. Mind maps are one approach to make such a system – you could do it on paper or in your mind. Regardless of whether you don't make a mind map, snowballing around a subject will unquestionably help structure more grounded recollections.

Consideration is critical to shaping recollections that are helpful:

The brain gets a great deal of data; a ton of it is pointless. Dealing with this data is hard. Consideration specifically picks data since it is important, helpful, sticking out, applicable, and so forth. Deliberately taking care of data gains shaping experiences simpler. Purposely notice things and take mental notes. Believe it or not, Attend to the data. Learning how to watch is a skill; with training, you can truly take care of data all around ok for it become a solid contender for memory arrangement.

The heaviness of data:

Data comes in a wide range of loads. By weight, I mean centrality. Some data is light and futile, and some data is substantial and helpful. You can intentionally regard some data as progressively significant by making it 'overwhelming.' This would prime your brain to solidify it during your REM cycle while dozing. Significant data asks the brain to remember it. The entirety of the above would help fortify the neural hardware associated with memory development just as help review that data better.

Fast deceives to improve the memory for explicit data:

These are exceptional stunts to help improve memory for explicit things. The past segment improves your general memory.

Mnemonics:

These are straightforward stunts that make data significant for the brain somehow or another. A few mental aides are straightforward, like making an abbreviation for an idea. Model – How to give great criticism? It ought to be Feed-forward, significant, brief, and convenient. A memory helper for this could be F.A.S.T. Some memory helper 'frameworks' require schoolwork, and they are amazing mental apparatuses.

1.The Major framework can be utilized to recollect numbers. Fundamentally, you relegate a fixed letter to each single-digit number and afterward utilize a blend of these letters dependent on the number you need to recollect by making words. Words are simple and significant, in this way, simple to recollect.

2.The mind royal residence (what Sherlock Holmes utilizes) is an exceptionally useful asset that influences the visuospatial memory circuits. Basically, one of the most dominant memory frameworks for the brain is the memory for the spatial area and its visual viewpoints. Consider it. How well would you be able to envision your home and the area of things in it? How well would you be able to recall your area? The mind castle is essentially a house/zone you know about. At each huge spot in the house or the territory, you 'place' data by making a relationship of that spot and the data. State my mind royal residence is my present house. Each room has protested in it, and I know their areas. I would then be able to begin at the passageway of my home and make the relationship of bits of data with each snippet of data. At that point, I can do likewise to another room. Etc; a mind castle can be gigantic. To review the data, I will essentially recollect the affiliations I made with every furniture thing and afterward extricate my data. With training, this gets simple.

3.The peg framework is genuinely simple. You can learn it quickly. The client makes fixed number-object affiliation, which we call 'pegs.' We, at that point, utilize this number-object pair to make a relationship with data. Along these lines, it is anything but difficult to review target data by recalling the peg and the affiliation. When the peg is known, one can right away tell the numerical situation of that data. To put it plainly, you fix an item you can envision with numbers 1 to 10. When you fix and gain proficiency with those (make it simple like one-sun, two – shoe, three - tree), basically partner data with that article through a clear creative mind. When you do that, you have a helpful instrument to recollect to-do assignments, glossary records, this answer, and so on.

Pieces:

This is a genuinely evident memory stunt; however, we regularly don't utilize it to its fullest. Piecing is a procedure to gather data into little assortments and treat the assortment as single units with data. State a telephone number – 43522350234 can be lumped as 435 – 223 – 502 - 34. You can piece things to purchase dependent on classes – stationary, meat, fluids, and so on. You can lump anything and make little units to recollect. Lumps are simple, arbitrary arrangements of long things are most certainly not. Ensure your groupings are little.

Great rest:

As referenced previously, learning and memory go connected at the hip with great rest. For recollections to shape, neural circuits need to keep up the data and fortify it through versatility. In the event that the data is helpful, significant, applicable in any capacity, the brain will carry out its responsibility and rebuild a tad to reinforce the circuits utilized for that data. This could be melodic practice, test answers, streets, and so on.

Make sure to recollect:

Maybe the simplest and most significant system. One basically reminds oneself that a specific piece of data is significant, and afterward, he/she reviews it. At the point when you make sure to recollect, you fundamentally increase the value of the data. When you really recollect that data, you do that once more. So, after some time, you would've practiced that data enough to be effectively accessible to you. You could recall the individuals you met at a meeting by rapidly repeating it in your mind. At that point, make sure to recall. After some time, you review the names. At that point, remind yourself once more. At last, after 3–4 times of doing that, you'd be realizing those names well.

Way of life viewpoints:

A general discovering is that having satisfactory

measures of Vitamin B12 is related to acceptable memory. Another discovering is that practicing 4 hours in the wake of examining merges that memory in the wake of learning superior to quick exercise. Customary rest is additionally connected with a better review. Keep in mind – learned data is a skill.

Attempting to review implies your brain is discovering its approach to start up that neural circuit that speaks to that data. That additionally implies that the 'reviewing' procedure can be fortified through training. So, a propensity for reviewing data will be valuable in extricating that data from your brain. It is outstanding amongst other investigation procedures – famously known as recovery practice.

Experience every one of these parts of memory cautiously. These methods will surely improve your general memory. The ability to recall is in your grasp!

STRATEGIES TO IMPROVE EMOTIONAL QUOTIENT IN THE WORK ENVIRONMENT

Giving indications of emotional intelligence in the workplace can improve your expert vocation significantly. Keeping up a high emotional intelligence EI at work can be fulfilling. It will doubtlessly assist you with sacking that since a long time ago pined for the contract, your supervisor has been pursuing since you can recollect. This gets conceivable with a mind with sufficient emotional intelligence. All things considered, securing and developing emotional intelligence can regularly be a hard errand to achieve since it takes a very long time of training and core interest. Likewise, procuring the best outcomes off can be hard to a dubious degree on the grounds that the vast majority are not ready to think straight when they are in a frightful spot. The accompanying focuses are going to help you improve emotional intelligence in every way that really matters:

A workplace is where individuals work for their manager, be its home office to a huge place of business or manufacturing plant.

Change is the main thing consistent on the planet. I trust everyone concurs with this announcement. Regardless of what your occupation is, the change will undoubtedly occur at your workplace.

The change can be in any way similar to the change of group elements, change of chief, change in the hierarchical chain of command, or technological changes, and these are just a couple to name. Just a genuinely versatile and adaptable individual can adapt to the progressions easily.

Significance of Emotional Intelligence in the Workplace:

The accompanying referenced are barely any reasons that clarify why emotional intelligence is valuable in the workplace.

1. Powerful association:
High emotional intelligence arms you with a

capacity of unconstrained and powerful association. This goes connected at the hip with workplaces that require consistent communication and persuading clients for the nature of items. More often than not, purchasers or sellers return frustrated on the grounds that retailers or sales reps can't have a viable discussion with them. Dealing with your EI or emotional quotient can assist you with evolving this. It does not just let you comprehend what others need or furtively want yet, in addition, enables you with the correct selection of words. Comprehending what to state in the midst of hardship is a help that can emerge out of high emotional intelligence.

2. Taking the path of least resistance:

Emotional intelligence at work keeps up the balance at work by imparting a reasonable methodology to the laborers. Unpracticed laborers in the prime of their childhood can be exceptionally hot-headed, and it is, without a doubt, a major misfortune for any organization. EI encourages you to deal with each issue with productive thoughtfulness. Not just that, it will likewise depict you in your most capable symbol. In some cases, purchasers filter through plenty of items requesting help with no expectation to purchase. So EI, will also bear on you by keeping up your cool or ready to help you to persuade the customers to purchase some things effectively.

3. Agreement:

Verifiably the idea of emotional intelligence brings mental harmony and congruity among laborers at the office. This is basic as laborers comprise a family, and a family must have tranquility. More often than not, the individual in charge isn't even around to keep an eye and ensure the laborers are quick to look after harmony. So, it is essentially on the workers to keep clashes and unsafe cross talks under control. In any case, it is impractical not to expect any issue or unsavoriness at work since it is a popularity-based nation, and everybody has an equivalent right to attest their will. In any case, emotionally develop individuals realize that the ideal path through work is to participate and be opposed during the unrest.

4. Taking into account the necessities:

Having a high emotional quotient is tied in with recognizing what is best for you and accomplishing your objective by comprehending what others need from you without their having said a word. It is a logical way that permits you to take into account impulses and intuit disposition and emotions heretofore in a fairly uncanny manner. In addition, it is actually what you need in a city where every single one is bringing home the bacon on the mystery. Well, this is a sort of mystery that gives you an advantage in any field of work. It lets you take changes sportingly and pick your activities appropriately. No different, increasing high emotional intelligence clears a path for all the great changes in your demeanor towards life and conduct.

5. An amazing interpretation of issues:

Emotional intelligence will prepare your mind to see past the unmistakable scope of mental sight. You will have the option to see twelve additional approaches to close a tricky issue where you needed to run from column to post on your days as a lesser human. It gives you an away from things that used to bewilder your mind prior to. In particular, you can peruse others' emotions and issues identified with it with no trouble. This is incredibly viable in issues of administrative lead...

Significance of Emotional Intelligence:

1. Sharpness:

Being emotionally savvy gives you a high turn in each issue. This is a consequence of improved readiness and dynamic awareness. High emotional intelligence works in a manner that prepares you to examine every single circumstance with accuracy and viability. EI cautions your sense to any condition giving you a legitimate understanding of the issue. This thus is answerable for faultless basic leadership and checks no mistake of judgment. Over everything, high emotional quotient opens you to a wide scope of bewildering mental abilities with which you can help other people, not to mention yourself.

2. Fast versatility:

In the midst of numerous characteristics, EI brings to the table, being adaptable to your condition is one of the most fulfilling. At the end of the day, you can never be shocked or lost base. You will consistently have something at your disposal to deal with. On the off chance that your work requests you to travel, at that point, this comes as an icing on the grounds that obviously you will wind up in a totally new environment than you were utilized to. I will, at that point, show you the best approach to win hearts at work in a total outsider region where not a spirit is known to you. Additionally, it very well may be helpful in a discussion while looking at arrangements. With your intuition top on, you won't just win exchanges yet additionally draw in more purchasers.

3. Getting a reasonable head:

Without an advanced mind, you can't get the exclusive requirements of living through your method for work. It is simply unrealistic on the grounds that all the fruitful individuals strolling the outside of earth have high emotional quotient. What's more, if that you need to be checked along that line, at that point, you should remove the mud from your head. Thinking boisterous and clear is the principal approach to guaranteed achievement. To right-minded individuals, any extreme state is only a day by day challenge they need to defeat to make a decent living. Also, individuals with high emotional intelligence make this look easy.

4. Being satisfactory:

In each circle of work, looking like it is profoundly basic to take care of business. Each road of work has a uniform. Regalia fills a need and shows cause. No different, high emotional quotient and satisfactoriness. In the event that you have not attired appropriately at work, you won't see a cheerful end to the day since the chances are that you will be passed over by clients themselves in the event that they can't place their confidence in you in view of the manner in which you look. Recognizing what to wear on specific days and how to establish a connection are two significant characteristics expected in a representative, and emotional intelligence prepares for you to acknowledge what you need.

5. Assurance:

Tirelessness and assurance are the way to progress. These two normal things can see you through a ton of jeopardizing circumstances. Anything shy of that includes some significant pitfalls of not being paid attention to by anybody. In this way, attempt to show guarantee at work and what preferred approach to do overthinking for high emotional intelligence. There are a ton of approaches to conducting yourself to a degree of empathy where you will have the option to handle issues all the more viably. In any event, persuading individuals gets simpler if your assurance is at top. These are only one stage away on the off chance that you are really moved to yield the gift of emotional intelligence.

Estimation of Emotional Intelligence in the Workplace:

1. The standard of self-guideline:

This is a vital prerequisite at work and is made conceivable by capable interpretation of issues by method for emotional intelligence. We, laborers, realize that it is so imperative to be very much educated on most recent patterns and items. Subsequently, self-guideline is an absolute necessity for every one of the individuals who try to arrive at a place sooner than later. Self-guideline implies being ready to be at standard with things that you are not all around familiar with. As it were, it implies that you should be fearless despite the threat. Also, to do so, you should ensure that you are not confounded. Practicing to improve upon your self-administrative skills by method for EI is an extraordinary method to use and run what you have accomplished.

2. Inspiration:

We are regularly used to get inspirational addresses from our supervisors because of our presentation. A few people are so strict about it that they start their day with an early morning portion of inspirational music to make them experience the dangers of the day. Ordinary many individuals search for a flash of inspiration though the appropriate response lies with themselves. In the event that you open a degree of high emotional intelligence, you will end up hitting upon the best plans to make you experience the day without feeling worked up in any capacity at all.

3. Care for other people:

When you can release the capability of emotional ability, you will have the option to see everything with a more clear vision and accuracy. Being emotionally enabled opens you to a universe of thoughtfulness that will assist you with associating with your encompassing better. Not exclusively will you start thinking about others to the extent that they start accepting you as one of their own. However, make you a commendable beneficiary of their generosity too. Besides, it does ponder on humanitarian grounds too since the world so far has a lot of savageries and can truly utilize a pinch of liberality.

Advantages of Emotional Intelligence in the Workplace:

1. Improves association with partners:

Your exhibition at the office essentially rotates around your association and association with your partners. Any messed-up correspondence can serious your ties with others in light of the fact that the location of modification is going to leave its blemish on your mind. Having high emotional intelligence not just encourages you to know not to lose your mind over something frivolous, yet in addition, shows you the genuine significance of safeguarding a blossoming association with your partners. Having companions at work pushes your enthusiasm for your work to new limits.

2. The perfect head:

Having a LARGE emotional intelligence at work can demonstrate really helpful with regards to sharpening your leadership characteristics. Everybody needs to admire a pioneer. So, you should show certain leadership attributes that will entrance others. This becomes simpler when you put your mind in carrying yourself satisfactory with your needs. Also, there is no preferred route over to oversee this, other than with your emotional ability. At exactly that point will you be viewed as a perfect chief for the general population. Besides, it will transform you into the individual to whom individuals would, for the most part, go to for help. Individuals will have the option to endow you with the privacy of their issues on the off chance that you give them confidence.

3. Positive turnaround:

Having high emotional intelligence gives you a positive bowed of mind. Individuals experiencing wretchedness and low self-regard have increased much from attempting to support the study of emotional intelligence. Things take a greatly improved turn once you make sense of how to channel your center onto a certain something, and that is to identify with others and see things through a perspective good for them and act as needs are. Aside from this, you will see a consistent ascent in your certainty.

Having said that, emotional intelligence, regardless of being fundamental at work, it is additionally crucially vital at each progression of life where this turns into the main factor for your own respectability. Additionally, this is one mantra you can aimlessly promise to live by, and the above tips and qualities in regards to emotional intelligence are unquestionably going to give you a reasonable point of view.

Sorts of Changes in the Workplace:

In this powerful condition, the association experiences a few changes; the following are to give some examples. Authoritative changes can be arranged into, for the most part, auxiliary, key, and individuals.

1. Change in the crucial vision of the organization:

When there is an adjustment in the management or when an organization is assumed to control over, change in crucial vision gets vital. All the association's choice is co-identified with it. This will be an all-inclusive change and influence every one of the workers.

2. Change in a hierarchical structure:

Post mergers and allegations, association experiences an adjustment in the structure. New management can plan to change practical and divisional structure to a level structure. This change can be tremendous for workers to adapt up to.

3. Change of individuals:

The exit of your preferred administrator or an associate who turned into your great companion can be a colossal change to survive. The other way around is additionally valid on the off chance that the number of new individuals in your area of expertise radically changes; at that point, it tends to be hard to adapt readily.

4. Change in approaches and legitimate understandings:

A little change in the arrangements or lawful understandings can make alarm among the representatives.

5. Change informs:

This change is one of the most widely recognized that an association faces. Regularly organizations think of new techniques that change the procedures followed in the association.

6. Change in innovation:

Associations regularly experience re-designing or mechanization, workers alarm as they feel their employments are in peril.

7. Joining:

At the point when a few changes in individuals, procedures, and structure happens, at that point incorporating everything together to turn out well is a major test for the change chief.

Why People Resist Change?

1. Loss of occupation:

With the presentation of any change representatives dread to lose their employment, they believe they will never again be required, or they may not conform to the change presented.

2. Not persuaded with the change:

Numerous representatives may accept that the present method for working is the best, and it requires no change. It is constantly recommended that upper management ought to transparently convey concerning why, how, when, who, and what effective result, the change can bring out. Be prepared for any inquiries that workers may have with respect to the new change and have an open entryway arrangement. Open and clear correspondence is the way to do change viably.

3. The dread of the obscure:

It is regular human nature to oppose change, and individuals feel good in the condition that is known to them. Individuals stick to the past, regardless of whether they realize the change can bring a great result.

4. Loss of control:

Recognizable circumstances, individuals, and procedures make work simple in this manner giving control over the workplace. At the point when change is presented, representatives feel befuddled and weak, which is likewise a reason why workers oppose change.

5. Poor competency:

Be it a basic, vital, or staff change in the association, everyone is required to upscale their skills and put in additional endeavors, yet numerous representatives are hesitant to adopt new things.

6. Such a large number of changes without a moment's delay:

Workers need time to adapt up to the progressions each in turn. Change must be presented when no other significant errand is inactivity; generally, individuals lose center and oppose change all the more unequivocally.

7. Interior utilized disagreement:

Any adjustment in the association will bring about bits of gossip about forecasts and antagonism when all is said in done. Additionally, rather than restricting the change, individuals contradict the individual who presented the change.

8. Loss of help:

Individuals will, in general, make great relations with supervisors and associates while getting to know each other at work, they know from whom they can look for help on occasion of difficulty. Any kind of individuals will break their emotionally supportive network.

How to Be More Flexible in the

Workplace?

1. Acknowledge that change occurs:

Be clear and acknowledge the way that change will undoubtedly happen regardless, change encourages you to learn and become consequently, one must grasp change with great enthusiasm.

2. Face your feelings of trepidation:

The vulnerability causes alarm. So, it is ideal for writing down your feelings of trepidation and consider your activity plan if that thing transforms into the real world. This makes you contemplate your own skills and capacities. Lucidity about yourself and your future will make you open and adaptable.

3. Know about the environment:

No change is unexpected. In the event that you are alert and a decent onlooker, you may get traces of the change that you may confront, scarcely any models could be – all gatherings of supervisors, manager acting removed, excluding you into gatherings. At the point when you get a few indications you can go top to bottom of the circumstance, along these lines, when change is presented, it won't come as a shock to you.

4. Perceive the phase of tolerating change:

When confronting change, individuals respond in the accompanying ways

Stage 1-Denial

At this stage, you will oppose change all together without pondering it. This is the absolute first stage post the declaration of the change.

Stage 2 – Anger

At this stage, you understand you can barely successfully stop the change, henceforth the feeling of outrage springs up. One gets uncertain, and the general circumstance gets clamorous

Stage 3 – Dejection

At this stage, outrage transforms into dissatisfaction. Individuals comprehend that they need to release things. As they acknowledge the way that change can't be halted, the feeling of outrage transforms into regret or frustration.

Stage 4 – Acceptance

This is where individuals begin to acknowledge the change and develop an uplifting standpoint towards it, they increase point of view, and it begins to reflect in their activities. Individuals at this stage quit being critical and gear up to acquire positive contributions for the association's development.

Stage 5 – Learning and development

At this stage, representatives are completely persuaded that the presented change is acceptable and was genuinely necessary. Here they choose to push forward. They understand what skills they can realize and how it will profit them later on. One can see expanded commitment and force in workers at this stage.

The time period to move from one phase to different changes from individual to individual, however on the off chance that management speaks with representatives regularly and workers themselves are open and adaptable, coming to organize five turns into a bit of cake. Be guaranteed that over the long haul, you will adapt up well to the change.

The sooner you arrive at the acknowledgment arrange; the simpler things will be for you.

5. Look for help:

We can't shroud our feeling and curb everything together, and it is encouraged to look for help and address your dear companions, partners, or relatives. These individuals can furnish you with direction and bolster, which can take you through intense occasions.

6. Impart, Communicate, And Communicate!!

It is futile to sit and sulk in dread simply. Rather, one ought to stand up to management and search for approaches to work things out. Be available to your interests and request arrangements. As much as the worker is concerned and dreading change, management is likewise confronting a test to get things settled. Procure an exact comprehension of the circumstance.

7. Be in an organization of the correct individuals:

There are five sorts of individuals in the hierarchical change

1. Pioneers:

These are the fiery arrangement of individuals who are eager to grasp change with great enthusiasm and are acutely intrigued for the change to happen. All the time, these are simply the individuals who are superior workers, sure, and have confronted changed before. They have a constructive encounter from their past change circumstances, and they know about how well it can assist an individual with growing and learn.

2. Obligators:

These individuals are eager to be a piece of a change and act excited on the grounds that they are approached to do as such by their supervisors, they are not content with the change, and yet they are not prepared to allow their manager to down, they proceed with their imagine game and sulk in dread.

3. Group Mentality:

These individuals won't have any solid supposition, and they are neither positive nor negative for transform; they want to pause and watch. In the event that they see the vast majority of the individuals restricting, they will join that group, and the other way around is likewise valid for these sorts of individuals.

4. Freethinkers:

The change will undoubtedly have a few bits of gossip and various assessments, a nonconformist won't be made a decision by any supposition, and he pauses and watches and afterward arrives at a resolution. His conclusion stands firm, and he likewise impacts the supporters with his perspectives. Management looks for such individuals and takes them in certainty. He can be a significant partner and a solid backer.

5. Couldn't care less disposition:

We can regularly discover a few people in the association who are least keen on vision and strategic the association, and neither do they care for their development and learning, they just work to gather their check and return home. These individuals won't respond to any change.

The association needs individuals who are proactive and can put additional endeavors to make things work. So, the workers falling in this classification are an aggravation for management; they are at a high hazard to get terminated.

It's upon you, who you need to be and with whom you ought to invest the greater part of your energy.

8. Question yourself in the event of dread:

Change your negative considerations into something positive. Think about when you dealt with change quite well, the cherished memory, a circumstance in your own relationship, or an issue you took care of at your workplace. Challenge at an individual and expert level is similarly hard to deal with.

In the event that you aced taking care of your issues in close to home life, you are essentially fit for comprehending the issue at your workplace. Introspect how might you deal with the change, by what means will you handle the correspondence, assess how the new change can bring out best in you. An individual's actual gauge can be made a decision in an upsetting and forced circumstance.

9. Quit shielding the change:

A few people pick up a go-moderate strategy. They become diverted from their work or express their wrath while working. Such conduct won't profit in any capacity; however, it may reverse discharge and demonstrate you as an amateurish. So, it is unequivocally proposed that, rather than protecting, grasp the change with great affection. you are not content with the change; you can transparently examine as opposed to dropping traces of the equivalent.

10. Be a piece of the change:

Associations require a few change pioneers who can fill in the void and perplexity produced by the change. You can be a piece of the change by including yourself in such exercises. Such activity can assist you in defeating your dread and give you the opportunity to eclipse. You can impact others by conveying the advantages of the change, can again assist you with building connections and improve your relational skills

11. Be sound and quiet:

To stay centered and face challenge circumstances, it is recommended to do some pressure easing exercises like Yoga and contemplation. These activities discharge feel-great hormones and cause you to feel vigorous. Aside from the activities, you can have a sound eating routine. Breathing activities and even a basic strolling of 20-30 minutes can assist you with freshening up your mind, in this way, expanding your ability of centering.

12. Act naturally motivated:

Rather than relaxing and trusting that things will settle down, you can concentrate on being progressively significant and upscaling your skills. Try not to get diverted and complete your assignments on schedule.

Hierarchical change isn't that difficult to adapt up to, it will undoubtedly occur, and everybody ought to be open and adaptable to adapt readily. With the correct demeanor, activities, and mindset, it is a simple method to cruise through.

What Makes a Great Workplace? Components and Characteristics

Your workplace resembles your sanctuary. It is where you dump your skills, your imagination, and your yields and get pride, bliss, and compensation consequently.

In any case, the grievous certainty is that very few individuals can appreciate the offices of having an incredible workplace. So, what makes a decent workplace?

What is a Great Workplace?

An extraordinary workplace alludes to a

positive domain where you get down to business consistently. It is where you feel regarded where your commitments are valued and where you appreciate cordial relational relations with your associates just as with your bosses.

If you need to make your workplace extraordinary, at that point, its pattern ought to be trusted. Trust among your workers drives incredible commitment among them along these lines improving business execution.

Likewise, such workplaces function admirably, bringing about incredible results. A portion of the measurements dependent on it is as per the following.

• 8% expansion in profitability

•16% development in overall revenue

•19% more noteworthy working pay

•50% fewer days off

•87% less inclined to leave the organization

•2.6 times EPS development (Earnings Per Share)

•12% higher client promotion

Great Working Environment Characteristics:

Extraordinary workplace, as a rule, has a couple of properties that cause them to vary from the ordinary kind of workplace.

These sorts of workplaces function admirably, and in addition, representatives love working in such workplaces.

The extraordinary workplaces are best in pulling in, maintenance, and great inspiring entertainers. Not many of the best credits and thoughts to improve the workplace are

•Provide representatives with testing works

•Invest more in preparing and development

•Recruit and hold the best workers

•Paying better remunerations or pay rates

•Motivate to oversee work/life balance

•Always worth and prize worker exhibitions

•Guide and offer help in developing top entertainers

•Take care of the representatives' wellbeing and health.

•Empower representatives

•We are maintaining a superior work culture.

•Share an association's exhibition with workers.

•Leaders ought to be rousing and extraordinary;

•Motivate towards advancement and development

•Recruiting the best workforce

Components of a Great Workplace:

An extraordinary workplace is a commitment of a few components cooperating. For a great many people, an extraordinary workplace would comprise of:

Security:

A sheltered space where you can contribute your thoughts and musings without feeling undermined or restless.

Great Relationships:

Where you can appreciate extraordinary relational associations with your bosses, your colleagues, and the staff working in the workplace.

Appreciation:

Where you are acknowledged for your commitments to the organization.

Assurance:

Where you have a sense of security and ensured to work.

Pride:

Where you feel gigantic pride in working.

Pay:

Where you are enough made up for your commitments.

Acknowledgment:

Where you are perceived for your great work and given due credit, you merit.

Trust:

Where you have trust and confidence in the individuals who you are working for.

Regard:

Where you feel regarded by the staff, your friends, and your managers.

Joining these above components, you can make an extraordinary working environment for yourself just as for your staff.

Qualities of a Great Workplace:

1. There is the open correspondence:

Probably the best quality of a workplace is one where you can appreciate straightforward and open correspondence.

Do you have a feeling that your words are approved at your workplace?

Do you get a reasonable opportunity to share your considerations, thoughts, and sentiments without the dread of being reproved?

Would you be able to go up to those in more

significant position authority and talk about an issue that has irritated you?

On the off chance that YES, at that point, congrats, you are working at an incredible workplace!

2. A decent work-life balance:

An incredible workplace isn't simply estimated by the amount you contribute to your workplace. It is likewise significant for you to keep a work-life balance.

This implies you in a perfect world ought not to be taking your work back home and work on the ends of the week. Realize when to state 'NO.'

A perfect work-life balance means that the workplace is an extraordinary workplace that realizes how to deal with their representatives' needs without overburdening them.

3. Practice collaboration, enjoy singularity:

One of the fundamental qualities of an

incredible workplace is one that soaks up in the entirety of their representatives a feeling of collaboration. You should feel great to work in a group with your collaborators. There ought to be no feelings of pessimism; rather, everybody should work as one towards a particular objective.

In any case, an extraordinary workplace is additionally one which permits you to grandstand your distinction. Perhaps you have an exceptional plan to add to this group venture. In the event that you are working at an incredible workplace, you will feel great to impart this plan to your different partners.

4. Excitement and camaraderie:

Does your workplace have an extraordinary camaraderie among the representatives?

Does everybody feel glad and positive working with one another in group ventures?

These are a portion of the indications of an incredible workplace. Everybody at the workplace is effectively progressing in the direction of a similar objective.

All of you may have various aspirations; however, so as to arrive at those desires, you have to cooperate as a group to accomplish set targets.

5. Fun:

An incredible workplace can't be basically described by the yields and benefits made by the organization. It is additionally a situation in which you anticipate visiting each day.

Being on acceptable terms with your colleagues is a certain something; however, developing workplace fellowships is substantially more uncommon. You ought to likewise realize how to have some good times at your workplace. On the off chance that your workplace appears to be an 'all work, no play' circumstance, at that point, you ought to be concerned.

6. Incredible individuals:

An incredible workplace is one that is comprised of extraordinary individuals. In the event that your workplace comprises of all the top laborers, dedicated people with imaginative minds, and dynamic characters, you are working at an incredible workplace.

A decent organization will contract and hold such individuals who can eclipse in each part of their work and their life.

7. Preparing and development:

An incredible workplace will effectively put resources into its representatives' preparation and development. The organization needs you to consistently overhaul your insight and skills to perform to your ideal level at the workplace.

So as to do as such, your organization makes the time, exertion, and open door for you to develop and develop your skills. A situation where you are continually learning new things and updating your insight can be viewed as an extraordinary workplace.

8. Wellbeing and welfare:
Your organization ought to put in overhauling your skills and information as well as in dealing with their individual workers. They do this by putting resources into your wellbeing and health by offering you healthier alternatives.

These choices cause you to teach a solid way of life and an extraordinary opportunity to be fit, sound, and positive.

9. Extraordinary leadership:

An extraordinary workplace is one that is

driven by incredible leaderships. In the event that your administrators and supervisors have incredible leadership characteristics, they regard every one of their workers.

Really check out their welfare and execution. A decent connection among workers and their pioneers comprise of shared regard, open correspondence, genuineness, and backing.

10. Offer back to society:

An extraordinary workplace can likewise be described by the amount they offer back to the network. The workplace ought to teach a propensity for surrendering to their representatives. They can do as such by giving their assets to philanthropy and serving the network by aiding those in need.

Privileged insights to Creating a Great Workplace:

While there are no mystical hacks that can assist you with making a situation of an extraordinary workplace, there are a few things you can do without anyone else to make a decent domain.

A portion of these tips and deceives can be begun quickly, and you will see the distinction in your workplace.

Straightforwardness and transparency:

Start instilling the propensity for being straightforward and open in the entirety of your exercises at your workplace. Regardless of whether this implies voicing out your disappointment at something said or done by a partner.

It is constantly a decent quality to be open and straightforward about your activities and feelings instead of discussing them despite somebody's good faith. This can make a vitiating air at the workplace.

Responsibility:

Show your responsibility towards your workplace, and you will receive the rewards. Give it your 100%, be it in a task, in a gathering, or at being a decent representative or chief.

Assume liability for your own behavior and words. You will have the option to make the climate of an extraordinary workplace thusly.

Giggle!

Giggling is the best drug! You don't have to keep up a genuine position at work consistently. Hotshot your stunning comical inclination and split a couple of jokes when the time and circumstance licenses you to do as such.

Chuckling is a characteristic pressure buster and discharges endorphins in your body, permitting you to keep working with an uplifting standpoint.

Adjust:

So as to make an incredible workplace condition, figure out how to be adaptable, and adjust to individuals and circumstances. As we as a whole know, change is the main consistent.

Being difficult or snobby in old thoughts will never permit you to push ahead, and all the more regularly, will make an awful working environment and distributed relationship.

Keep up a parity:

Realize when to state 'NO.' In the event that you need to work at an incredible workplace, you have to begin making the strides alone. Keeping up a decent work-life balance is basic in doing as such.

You have to figure out how to land at work early and go home on schedule. Realize when you have to simply stop, consider it daily and return home and invest energy with your family. A decent close to home life is equivalent to a crisp mind and a decent work-life.

Communicate:

It is significant for you to communicate with everybody at your workplace while keeping up a specific degree of polished skill. Your activity isn't just to find a workable pace, your assignments, and leave.

Develop great relational associations with your companions and other staff individuals. This offers an approach to making a cheerful and serene workplace.

Keep your workers locked in:

An incredible workplace is one where your representatives are constantly occupied with a movement. On the off chance that work isn't accumulating, make some reality for everybody to unwind and simply take a break work.

Participate in entertainment only and intriguing exercises. You can likewise have workshops at the workplace with the goal that the staff can learn or develop another and fascinating skill. This will keep everybody at the workplace constantly connected with, dynamic and cheerful.

Meritocracy:

Probably the greatest mystery to an incredible workplace is to advance meritocracy. Pay and award based on a chain of command advance a negative situation at the workplace, where other persevering representatives feel uncalled for at not being given the proper compensation for their exertion.

Rather, let everybody realize that they will be reasonably compensated for their difficult work, and the organization will develop by a wide margin while keeping up a solid workplace condition.

Cheerful characters:

What appears the clearest approach to teach energy into the workplace?

It is by filling the workplace with glad, constructive, and idealistic individuals.

Keep governmental issues as far away as would be prudent and keep up separation with the individuals who like to stay in such a domain. Rather, figure out how to carry on with a sound life and be sure, so you can spread this inspiration at your workplace.

Try not to be cruel:

It is conceivable that somebody has accomplished something at the workplace which you don't appreciate.

Notwithstanding, it is significant that you recall not to be cruel. Regardless of whether you should differ with another person, do as such without disregarding or putting them down.

Escape the groove:

Perhaps the greatest mystery to making an extraordinary workplace is to escape the schedule now and again and figure out how to live outside of the workplace.

Make an arrangement to go out someplace with all your office staff for an end of the week, perhaps to a football match-up, or the carnival, or simply out for a night of beverages.

This trip can end up being solid as it will reinforce the bond between associates at the workplace just as allow everybody to find a good pace other and have a fabulous time in an alternate sort of a situation. This activity can likewise help in building a solid bond and a feeling of camaraderie among workers.

Having extraordinary work to anticipate each morning can probably be the best thing in your life. You will have the option to put forth a strong effort, develop stunning connections, and watch your vocation soar. Making an incredible workplace begins from inside, so follow a portion of these basic privileged insights to making an extraordinary workplace and anticipate Monday's for a mind-blowing remainder.

CONCLUSION

Our Emotional Quotient (EQ) item takes a gander at an individual's emotional intelligence, which is the capacity to detect, comprehend and adequately apply the force and intuition of emotions to encourage more significant levels of coordinated effort and efficiency.

This book incorporates practical and hypothetical guides and techniques to Knowing one's emotions, Controlling one's emotions, Recognizing emotions in others (empathy), Controlling emotions in others, Improvement in emotional control.

Emotional Intelligence holds the best five space on the most searched for after business skills. Organizations need to contract people who can manage weight and kick off something new.

What's more, remembering that adding Emotional Intelligence to your overview of skills will without a doubt make you progressively appealing, that isn't all it's advantageous for: it is moreover a skill that everyone needs in our step by step lives and is obviously more huge than one's QI or other particular limits concerning choosing a person's general achievement for the duration of regular day to day existence.

Emotional Intelligence (EQ) or Emotional leftover portion is obviously more noteworthy than one's intelligence leftover portion or practical limits with respect to choosing a person's general achievement for the duration of regular daily existence. Emotional intelligence clearly impacts how we detail individual decisions, the manner in which we oversee lead, and our ability to travel through social complexities. The unprecedented thing is, emotional intelligence is something that everybody can make with time. This guide will give every one of you the central learning expected to improve your EQ.